FINDING TOKEN CREEK

OTHER BOOKS BY ROBERT ALEXANDER

Poetry

What the Raven Said

White Pine Sucker River

Nonfiction

*The Northwest Ordinance: Constitutional Politics
and the Theft of Native Land*

Five Forks: Waterloo of the Confederacy

Anthologies

*Spring Phantoms:
Short Prose by 19th Century British & American Authors*
ed. Robert Alexander

*Nothing to Declare:
A Guide to the Flash Sequence*
ed. Robert Alexander, Eric Braun, and Debra Marquart

*Family Portrait:
American Prose Poetry, 1900-1950*
ed. Robert Alexander

*The House of Your Dream:
An International Collection of Prose Poetry*
ed. Robert Alexander and Dennis Maloney

*The Party Train:
A Collection of North American Prose Poetry*
ed. Robert Alexander, Mark Vinz, and C. W. Truesdale

Robert Alexander

Finding Token Creek

New & Selected Writing, 1975–2020

WHITE PINE PRESS / BUFFALO, NEW YORK

White Pine Press
P.O. Box 236
Buffalo, NY 14201
www.whitepine.org

Publication of this book was supported by public funds from the New
York State Council on the Arts, with the support of Governor Andrew
M. Cuomo and the New York State Legislature, a State Agency.

Printed and bound in the United States of America.

Cover painting: *Canard à l'Orange* by Anne Kessler.
Copyright © 2011 by Anne Kessler

ISBN 978-1-945680-44-1

Library of Congress Control Number: 2020930088

for Katie

Contents

from *What the Raven Said*

from *White Pine Sucker River*

from *Five Forks: Waterloo of the Confederacy*

Postscript

FINDING TOKEN CREEK

Oh, and I have watched you, fish
of heaven, here in Wisconsin . . .

—Jim Hazard

About a month past the equinox, mid-morning, the lake is empty save for a couple of grebes who follow me along, keeping their distance. (It seems the grebes are always the last birds to stop by the lake on their autumn journey.) Then down by the end of the lake, perhaps a mile away, I see what looks to be a ghost canoe with two paddlers. As I slowly progress south, stroke by stroke, they appear to mirror my progress northward, approaching me. By the time I get close to the little stream I call Frog Creek, I can see them clearly—a pair of swans. We are all there on the morning lake: two swans, two grebes, and me.

The morning fog has left droplets in the branches and few remaining leaves along the creek, stretching up to where it bends out of sight. I turn for home. The grebes pass off into the middle of the lake and the swans continue to follow me north. Then I hear behind me the sound of feathers being dragged along water, and when I turn to look I see the swans beating southward just above the surface of the lake. I watch them as they slowly gain altitude—until finally, two white specks above the low ridge to the south, they merge into the autumn sky.

Prose/Poetry

What is poetry and if you know what poetry is what is prose.
—Gertrude Stein

For years I wrote prose poems without knowing what I was doing, thinking instead that I was writing some sort of shrunken, deformed story that I was too lazy to transform into a piece of *real* fiction. At the time, *prose poem* to me meant some sort of Dada-esque stream-of-consciousness vignette—and I, on the other hand, was writing what I thought of simply as very short stories. This was long before the term *flash* had been applied to fiction in any but a marketing sense, and *short shorts* still referred to an item of clothing.

For a while I told anyone who would listen that I was writing, or attempting to write, "experimental fiction." While it was true that some of these pieces, put together as a sequence, did hint at an underlying theme, a montage-like connection of some sort between the disparate sections, in a traditional sense they lacked pretty much all semblance of a plot. So it wasn't long before I felt uncomfortable calling them fiction at all and began writing sentences which were broken up into lines—that is, *free verse*. But this wasn't satisfying either. I kept feeling self-conscious, as though the words I was putting on the page were announcing themselves as POETRY—and I had to keep thinking of how and where to end the line, or of how it would seem if I didn't end it but instead began to sound like Blake or Whitman or Ginsberg. No, that wasn't what I wanted at all. I wanted to write *prose,* thank you very much.

One day, I decided to come out of the closet and to admit that, yes, I was writing prose poems—but then to add, *sotto voce:* Though perhaps they're not what you've come to think of as prose poems. I wasn't sure at the time that many people in America had come to think much at all about the prose poem, but by God I knew what I thought of it. It gave me the freedom to play with a mix of characteristics of tone and style and subject matter that were traditionally the realm of fiction writers, along with other elements that were traditionally poetic. That was the key to me: to be able to draw on the resources available to both fiction writers and poets.

The impulse of prose, it seems to me, is to tell a story—a story grounded in the real world—and this is true whether we are writing (or reading) a newspaper article, a letter, a biography, or a novel. Prose can therefore speak of everyday experience in ways difficult if not impossible for free verse. This ability of the prose poem to take on various registers of language, its ability to masquerade as different sorts of literary or non-literary prose, is one of its distinguishing characteristics—what Margueritte Murphy calls (after Mikhail Bakhtin) its *heteroglossia.*[1] In this way, prose contains the language of the everyday—but a poem is something else again. When we break a paragraph up into lines, creating free verse, the text immediately does more than simply tell a story. The context has shifted. The poem takes on airs, it has pretensions. Prose says: "Come listen. I alone can tell this tale." But a poem entices us: "Come listen. No one else can tell this tale as artfully as I."

To get an idea of how this distinction actually works in practice, it's instructive to look at a piece of writing that has appeared in print as both poetry and prose. In his introduction to *The Oxford Book of Modern Poetry,* W. B. Yeats briefly discusses Walter Pater's influence on the post-Victorian generation. Pater, as Yeats says, "was accustomed to give each sentence a separate page of manuscript, isolating and analyzing its rhythm"—and, therefore, "only by printing it in *vers libre* can one show its revolutionary importance."[2] This Yeats does, presenting a lineated version of a sentence in which Pater describes Michelangelo's *Mona Lisa:*

First, here's the original:

She is older than the rocks among which she sits;
like the vampire, she has been dead many times,
and learned the secrets of the grave; and has been
a diver in deep seas, and keeps their fallen day
about her; and trafficked for strange webs with
Eastern merchants; and, as Leda, was the mother
of Helen of Troy, and, as Saint Anne, the mother
of Mary; and all this has been to her but as the
sound of lyres and flutes, and lives only in the del-
icacy with which it has molded the changing lin-
eaments, and tinged the eyelids and the hands.[3]

And here is Yeats' lineated version of this sentence:

She is older than the rocks among which she sits;
like the vampire,
she has been dead many times,
and learned the secrets of the grave;
and has been a diver in deep seas,
and keeps their fallen day about her;
and trafficked for strange webs with Eastern merchants;
and, as Leda,
was the mother of Helen of Troy,
and, as Saint Anne,
was the mother of Mary;
and all this has been to her but as the sound of lyres and flutes,
and lives
only in the delicacy
with which it has molded the changing lineaments,
and tinged the eyelids and the hands.[4]

Yeats has added one word, "was," at the beginning of the eleventh line, presumably because the rhythm, as free verse, is slightly different in this case from the prose version. This rhythmic difference arises because the line ending causes a typical reader, on a subtle or not-so-subtle level, to slow the pace down and emphasize the individual words of the clause, requiring a second "was" to support the repetition.

One effect of the lineation, in other words, is to add another kind of punctuation. Denise Levertov, in speaking of this phenomenon, says that

> The most obvious function of the line-break is rhythmic:
> it can record the slight (but meaningful) hesitations between
> word and word that are characteristic of the mind's dance
> among perceptions but which are not noted by grammatical
> punctuation.[5]

In this way lineation leads to a different sort of stress pattern in free verse than occurs in prose. As Alice Corbin Henderson stated in 1913, while assistant editor of Harriet Monroe's newly-fledged *Poetry* magazine, "The essential difference between prose and poetry is in the quality of the rhythmic phrase."[6] This difference comes to the ear as a higher ratio of stressed to unstressed syllables in the lineated version of Pater's sentence than in the prose. Investigating just this difference in a dissertation study at the University of Wisconsin–Milwaukee, Prudence Byers examined how people read aloud different kinds of non-metrical texts. She measured, among other things, the number of stressed and unstressed syllables in each sample. As it turns out, the ratio of stressed to unstressed syllables in free verse is, not surprisingly, higher than in prose.[7] Thus it's possible to say that one characteristic which distinguishes free verse rhythms from those of prose is an increased frequency of stress. The lines, like blank verse, can begin to sound incantatory.

If not iambic itself, free verse plays itself off against the deeply-felt iambic rhythm of blank verse—the other unrhymed poetry in English. Free verse is haunted thus by the ghost of blank verse, and its shackles are difficult to throw off.

Highly stressed language also sounds more British than American. As Henry Mencken says in *The American Language*, "In general, the speech-tunes of the Englishman show wider melodic curves than those of the American, and also more rapid changes."[8] In effect, this comes across as speech with a greater number of stressed syllables—again, more like blank verse than prose. Though this works for British speech, it's hard to render the rhythms of the American language in an iambic line. "We do not speak English—remember that," said William Carlos Williams: "We speak our own language."[9] And therefore we need a poetry of our own, one that contains the American voice as well as blank verse (together with its free verse variations) contains the English voice. What we have in the prose poem is a piece of writing grounded in the real world, whose rhythms and intonations embody not a traditional English prosody, but rather the speech patterns of everyday America. And therefore, in my opinion, the prose poem is a form particularly suited to American poetry.

*　　*　　*

Though many poems are fictional, this doesn't make them fiction in the sense that term is generally used. In the common understanding, a piece of fiction must have a plot, though in a one-page fiction the plot might be only implied or presumed. Plot in a "normal" piece of fiction—story, novel, film—involves the working-through of some sort of interpersonal tension over a span of time. In a short-short, the resolution can only be hinted at: the process caught in a single frame, contained in one precise moment.

On the one hand, a traditional narrative is built up by slow degrees, layer by layer of impressions like an Old Masters oil painting; on the other hand, flash fiction is like Zen calligraphy, all the creative energy stored like water behind a dam—or electricity in a Leiden jar—released in one burst of activity, lines on paper, the sense of the thing captured in just a few quick strokes. There are works of verse that operate this same way, but we conceive of them as poems rather than stories. Take, for example, Shakespeare's sonnets, which interweave the Narrator, his Beloved, and the mysterious Other Man. If written in prose, these could make a flash sequence—each individual piece capturing a single emotional configuration—but they are sonnets, and we focus less on the implied or hidden "plot" and more on the writing itself, each piece shining with what Walter Pater, in another context, called a hard, gem-like flame.

A plot means simply that something *happens* within a story, while in a poem all we can say for sure is that something *is happening*. In fact this is only a question of emphasis. The novel, or story, concerns itself with what physicists call the *arrow of time*—or the arc which any particular arrow follows—while the poem, or lyric, concerns itself with what Buddhists might call the *suchness* of time, the way that things manifest in the moment. Often a piece of writing will do both, and it's a toss-up as to which is predominant—but to the reader, emphasis can often be seen as essence, what the text in question is really "about."

So what's the difference between a prose poem and a short-short story? I think the question itself reveals a misapprehension. Like the legendary blind men examining an elephant, each one of us feels the particular part of the body he or she is holding, and no one agrees with the others as to what sort of creature it is that they're touching. Like tribes with different sorts of kinship relations, we argue over what to call the child who's the son or daughter of a mixed marriage. But it's the same kid we're talking about—and let's not forget that. The question itself presupposes a duality or opposition, a this-or-that relationship in which there exists a certain boundary between the two forms, *poem* and *story*. But in fact many pieces of prose can be conceived as falling into both categories, and in those cases, at least, this is a distinction without a difference. They are two sides of a single coin.

Each reader, I'm suggesting, is responsible for accounting for a particular piece of writing in his or her own way; the act of reading thus defines the text. In its essence the short prose piece, by whatever name, is a hybrid form, located at the crossroads of story and poem. On the one hand we can trace its lineage back through the universe of poetry—rhymed verse, blank verse, free verse—and on the other hand its background includes the whole world of prose—fiction, nonfiction, memos and letters home. Those who call what they write *flash fiction* see themselves as heirs of a whole tradition of storytellers, and those who write *prose poems* see themselves in a long line of poets. The reality, of course, is that poets are, many of them, storytellers—just as storytellers, many of them, are poets. Both schools have ended up being drawn to the same classroom, short prose, but each sees that *short* as a different sort of place.

The story, whatever name it takes, has as part of its charm that it's written in what we can call the language of the quotidian, language that purports to tell of the real world. Poetry, on the other hand, by its very nature exists beyond the realm of ordinary discourse—and this combination of opposites is what makes the prose poem so endlessly fascinating. While prose rises organically from the everyday, poetry with its long tradition of "nightingales and psalms" has about it something transcendent—something, we might say, of the sacred. In this way the prose poem, child of two worlds, serves to bring together, at long last, the sacred and mundane.

More than a century ago, Walt Whitman wrote: "In my opinion the time has arrived to essentially break down the barriers of form between prose and poetry." The muse of America, he concluded, "soars to the freer, vast, diviner heaven of prose."[10]

[1] Margueritte S. Murphy, *A Tradition of Subversion: The Prose Poem in English from Wilde to Ashbery* (Amherst: Univ. of Massachusetts Press, 1992), 90.

[2] W.B. Yeats, Introduction to *The Oxford Book of Modern Verse, 1892–1935* (New York: Oxford University Press, 1936, viii.

[3] Walter Pater, *The Renaissance: Studies in Art and Poetry* (London, 1888), 130.

[4] Walter Pater, "Mona Lisa," *The Oxford Book of Modern Verse*, 1.

[5] Denise Levertov, "On the Function of the Line" [1979], *New and Selected Essays* (New York: New Directions, 1992), 79.

[6] Alice Corbin Henderson, "Poetic Prose and Vers Libre," *Poetry* 2.2 (May 1913), 70.

[7] Prudence P. Byers, "The Contribution of Intonation to the Rhythm and Melody of Non-Metrical English Poetry" (Ph.D. diss., Univ. of Wisconsin–Milwaukee, 1977), 31; see also Tables 18 and 19, pp. 41–42.

[8] H.L. Mencken, *The American Language*, Fourth Edition (New York: Knopf, 1936), 322.

[9] William Carlos Williams, "Briarcliffe Junior College Talk," as quoted in Linda Welsheimer Wagner, *The Prose of William Carlos Williams* (Middletown: Wesleyan Univ. Press, 1970) 8.

[10] Walt Whitman, "Notes Left Over," *Collected Prose*, vol. 2 of *Complete Poetry and Prose* (1892; New York: Farrar, Straus & Giroux, 1968), 332–333.

Richmond Burning

Clouds of Swallows

The swallows arrive sometime after mid-April and nest along the bluffs. They ignore me as I canoe past, twittering around my head as they leap and spin in search of breakfast, pausing singly or in pairs for a brief moment (resting on a ledge or on a branch) before rejoining the hunt. At times I see them sitting on their nests, small bowls of mud and grass stems held together, like papier-mâché, with dried saliva, lined with downy breast feathers. I wonder how many mouthfuls of mud it takes, and how many hours, for a swallow to build her nest. If I get too close they fly off, and I can just see, if I let my canoe touch the cliff and I sit up very straight, a small brown egg in its cradle of down.

Today there are swallows flying all around me. Something catches my eye. I see two swallows together fluttering downward through the air. There's one atop the other, and I'm beginning to get the sense of it—one holding the other in his wings, a confused motion toward the water below. (I've never before seen swallows more than touch the surface in flight.) They settle to the water's surface, and he's still holding on, seeming to pull her up and down— and as I start to fear she'll drown, he finishes and flies off. She is floating now on the water's surface, resting, her wings spread out on either side; then suddenly she shakes her wings and seems to leap from the surface of the lake, flying off to rejoin the cloud of swallows crossing back and forth beneath the limestone bluffs.

Maggie May

I can't remember the pretense by which the two of us, after dinner, had ended up in the barn, rather her freckles are what I remember and the prickliness of the hay through the gray wool blanket, the late summer sunlight coming in through the hayloft door and her face above me framed in the dust which moved ever so slightly in the sunbeams.

It was the year that Rod Stewart sang about Maggie May and there I was going back to school with the field corn drying in September. I was going to be a world-class novelist and this was the year it would happen, me holed up in a farmhouse outside of town with wood heat and a small writing desk beneath the window that overlooked alfalfa fields and the oak-scattered hills.

It didn't happen that way. I never saw her again and the novel I wrote ended up serving for the most part to ignite the wood in the stove. It was a long winter with a particularly severe ice storm that left the tops of the trees for miles around broken off—you'd see them for several years afterward, remnants of the glittering destruction. School was called off for a week as the power was down in several counties. It was mid-February and warmer than usual but still we were lucky we had the woodstove.

Many years later her by-then-ex-husband was a lot richer and I had to write to him hat in hand, soliciting for a small press that I had helped run into the ground. I had seen him only once after that evening in the hayloft: sitting on the terrace at the Student Union, overlooking the clear October lake, holding forth with a group of grad students about Blaise Cendrars. I wondered if he knew I'd had a hook-up with his wife, as he barely caught my eye.

It wasn't in surrealist literature he made his money but rather medicine—a self-styled Bill Williams of the prairies. By this time our press was down to its last round of letters, begging for one more hand-out to get us through the lean years; he had divorced her and remarried, had cashed in his investments and was living on the west coast. For a rich guy, yachts and ponies, he sent us a pittance. Along with a note: *Don't ask again.*

Late One Night

The air was literally filled with Pigeons; the light of noon-day was obscured as by an eclipse, the dung fell in spots, not unlike melting flakes of snow; and the continued buzz of wings had a tendency to lull my senses to repose. . . . Before sunset I reached Louisville, distant from Hardensburgh fifty-five miles. The Pigeons were still passing in undiminished numbers, and continued to do so for three days in succession.

—John Audubon

Late one night, just days after midsummer, letting the dog out one last time before going to bed, I turn on the outside light then open the door to the evening fog. Drops glisten on the black wrought-iron table. My dog barks, a bird utters a sound of surprise and flies up from beside the water bowl, alights on the teak bench (my dog ignores her, walks to the edge of the deck).

I notice the bird's long neck, iridescent in the fog: a pigeon I've never seen before, larger than a mourning dove. The bird watches me but doesn't move as I walk to the edge of the deck and my dog steps down to pee in the dune grass (Lake Superior, a hundred yards to the north, is silent in the fog), then we slip back inside and I close the door softly, turn out the light.

In the morning the bird is gone, and I check the bird book, see a picture of a passenger pigeon—"now extinct"—looking back at me.

Frog-Pond in April

It's the first warm day this year—not hot, but warm—which is to say it's the first warm day in six months. None of the trees have leaves yet—it still looks like autumn, brown and bare—but it's warm, and there are bright green and yellow spots of daffodils, and open areas where the grass is green. Because of the world-wide die-off of frog species he's read about, Ralph a couple of weeks back put a black molded plastic two-feet-in-diameter frog-pond under a cedar, where it will be protected from sunlight that's presumably (with the hole in the ozone layer) destroying with ultraviolet many fragile unprotected frog-eggs hanging silent and vulnerable in their translucent white foam.

Late that afternoon, after finishing his chores, Ralph's sitting on his porch halfway up the hillside, looking down at the frog-pond, and a sparrow comes to bathe while the late afternoon sun falls across the water. She splashes herself and throws off a sheen of drops. After a few minutes of this—Ralph glances up to see a hawk circling above— after a few minutes of splashing the sparrow jumps *into* the water and is up to her neck and then she's under water, head and all—and then jumps out of the water, fluffs up and shakes on the edge of the frog-pond and then flies up to a low branch of the cedar where she continues drying and preening.

Just on time, it seems, a male sparrow appears on the branch and the two birds fly off together—while far above them the red-tail hawk, looking for bigger game, continues to turn and soar.

Afternoon

A bright afternoon, and late enough in the year that the sun has moved out of the shadow of the trees and casts a welcome warmth on the calm water, so calm the clouds are reflected beneath me and it's as though I'm paddling in the middle of the sky. A couple of cedars have fallen where the bank collapsed a year ago, making a tangle of brush. As I lift my paddle I hear a rustling in the branches. Looking closer, I see a small shape, dark brown fur, and then the mink stops not three feet away, looking at me, a splash of white on its chin like a cat who's been lapping cream. As I start to paddle again the mink follows me, scrambling in and out of roots and tangles, small clawed feet slipping on the wet rocks along the shoreline. Sun in the sky and scattered clouds on the water's surface, we head toward twilight and the south end of the lake.

Richmond Burning

When I met her she was wearing on the lapel of her vest, where a carnation or a political button might go in election years, a two-inch image of Jupiter. This was a Halloween party but the button and vest were her only costume, unless you count her chicory-blue eyes and the purple leotard she had on beneath her vest.

"What's with Jupiter," I asked the woman whose name I had not yet learned.

"Abundance," she said. "Jupiter signifies abundance."

"I could use some of that," I told her. Her blue eyes were abundance enough for me. Shortly after that, a couple of beers beneath our belts, we went back to my apartment, the upstairs of a small story-and-a-half, to walk my dog around the block and get to know each other better, to set our costumes aside.

*   *   *

The couple leaving the Richmond airport looked from a distance like many at this time of year, dressed for Christmas vacation, a casual but slightly dressy air that signifies dinner with family and, a day later, a half-hour spent opening presents beside a well-lit tree. She wore an alpaca scarf which lay lightly on her leather coat, and he an overcoat that looked as though it could have come off one of the Confederate statues on Monument Avenue. Which is to say it appeared an even shade of gray, the sparse colored threads of the Harris tweed blending into the gray warp and weft.

After picking up their rental car, they drove from the airport, by the old Confederate fortifications (only a few cannon and mounds of earth remaining from the fifty-mile dike which, for nearly four years, held back the Yankee tide)—and headed on the empty expressway to their hotel downtown, on the south side of Capitol Square. This being Christmas eve, all the politicians had gone back to their wives and families, leaving their mistresses for the more tedious distractions of home: wrapping Christmas presents, trimming the tree, attending the seasonal caroling at the local school or church. Hence there were suites available at a heavily-discounted rate, less than the usual cost of a single room, which the husband appreciated, his wife having expensive and not-often-satisfied tastes. The trade-off was this: for the cost of a single room facing the Capitol, you could have a suite of back rooms with no view at all.

It was the only hotel that he had ever been in where—instead of a mini-bar stocking those tiny bottles of booze that airlines sell their passengers—the bottom drawer of the customary hotel dresser was filled with an assortment of pints and half-pints of whiskey. Here he saw an eminent example of traditional Virginia smoking-room politics, played out over a deck of cards.

*   *   *

That year I spent most afternoons in the rare book reading room of the university library, paging through brittle copies of literary magazines dating from the early years of the twentieth century. In the early evening I'd leave the library and return to my sorrowful dog in my upstairs apartment, and then after dinner she of the purple leotard would show up with a bottle of wine, climb the backstairs of the house and knock on my door. I will spare myself the pain of voyeuristically reliving the sweet details, from a time so long gone, and leave the erotica to the reader's imagination.

*   *   *

A short time later darkness had fallen and the couple left the hotel and walked across the street to their rental car parked alongside Capitol Square, which was enclosed by a dark iron fence. Inside was the massive form of Jefferson's white Capitol, façade lit by spotlights, surrounded by oaks whose fallen leaves lay in the gutter by the car. The temperature was around freezing and there were spots of ice among the leaves. In normal times there wouldn't have been a parking place for blocks around, but this Christmas eve all was quiet as they stepped gingerly across the fallen oak leaves.

It was, given the empty streets, a shorter drive than usual to her adoptive mother's house in Henrico County. It is a peculiarity of Virginia that certain "independent" cities lie like separate islands within their surrounding counties. Thus there were no sheriffs patrolling the city streets and it was unusual, in certain neighborhoods, to see a traffic cop at all. The police had their hands full elsewhere, Richmond being one hub of a bustling trade in which drugs from New York City were brought south and exchanged for firearms where gun laws were more lax.

*   *   *

We shared our stories with each other. Dropping out of college, she'd left for California years before. Now she was back and planned to spend the winter living in a friend's apartment on the East Side, studying astrology with a guy who had a slot on a local radio show. She told me she had fallen in love with her voice instructor in college—who was, as I recall, already married—and had become pregnant with his child. He never learned that she gave birth to a baby girl. In California she had put their child up for adoption.

*   *   *

Later, he would look back at that dinner as the opening scene in the final act of his marriage. His mother-in-law was there, and her sister—and the neighbor from across the street, a woman twenty-some years their junior, who drove the van when they all went on excursions to Charlottesville. "I miss the summers here," his wife said, "when you lie in bed at night and your body's covered by a thin layer of sweat." He remembered cicadas and honeysuckle, a slight breeze through the willow oak in the backyard.

*   *   *

Like all such things this couldn't last, and didn't. By January we had burned each other out and she left for California. The winter in Wisconsin and the memories of her home above the Russian River had sent her westward once again.

I followed her out there on my spring break—I remember flying over the snow-covered Sierras shining beneath a full moon—and for a couple of weeks we lived together in an old wine vat with a roof of sliding Plexiglas panels, perched on the side of a mountain. We opened the panels to the madrona trees and redwoods, to cloudless sky. I began investigating the possibility of teaching at a local college.

One morning my lover told me it was her daughter's birthday. She carried that sadness within her—probably one thing that so attracted me to her—and each

34

year, on that particular day, it rose and nearly swamped her.

At the college they told me they could have their choice of any poet they wanted in the Bay area—so why would they choose me? I returned to my apartment and my little magazines, while the Wisconsin spring began in its slow way to flower the landscape. Soon I finished my degree and quit teaching altogether. And my California friend I saw only once again, a few years later, when she was back for a brief visit and we went out for breakfast. Her eyes were as blue as I remembered.

*   *   *

Back in their hotel room the first thing she did, after taking off her coat, was to pour herself a drink from the half-filled pint of Maker's Mark.

"So where is it?" she asked him.

He had worried about it all through both airports, going through security in Madison and then again walking through the airport in Richmond. He always worried when he carried weed on a plane, though in those far off days before 9/11 security was a spotty affair at best. But there was always the chance a butterfly could flap its wings in Mexico and his suitcase would fall off the conveyor belt and split open on the tarmac, and his rolled-up socks fall out for all to view .

"I'm saving it for Christmas," he said. "Something special for Santa."

She slapped him hard across the mouth. His lips stung, and he tasted blood from where her wedding ring had caught him.

"Fuck you," he told her. "You can wait until tomorrow." She slapped him again. And then she closed her fist and hit him in the face.

*   *   *

In the meantime the father of her child had become a public figure. The local chamber music society, which he conducted, began playing a series of public concerts downtown during the summer months. Every Wednesday evening at these "Concerts on the Green" a local French restaurant provided box picnics for people drinking wine out on the lawn.

*   *   *

It wasn't the first time she'd gotten violent. He'd been advised to stay away until the rage subsided. This time it was a suite they were in, and there was a second bedroom— so he went into the second room, closed the door and put the little hook through the metal loop on the doorjamb. He took his shoes off and lay down on the bed fully dressed. She broke the door open, the eye-bolt flying off the splintered doorjamb, and the door swept open and there she was in the room. He stood up from the bed and she threw the heavy cocktail glass at his head and it smashed against the wall, and glass suddenly covered the floor. She was hitting him in the face. He pushed her away and backed out into the main room of the suite and went to the telephone.

Trying to fend her off with one hand and hold the receiver in the other, he called the front desk and told the guy his wife had flipped out and he needed another room. All the time his wife is yelling, "Where's the goddamn pot, just tell me where's the goddamn pot."

He took his suitcase from the closet and started trying to stuff his clothes in—shirts, pants, jacket, shoes—and then there was a knock at the door and a young guy stood there waiting. His wife, calming down in a hurry as she could when she wanted to, started telling the guy that things were really just fine and her husband was acting crazy. She remained behind while he dragged the suitcase down the hall to the elevator. He hadn't managed to zip the suitcase all the way up and there were pieces of clothing sticking out through the open zipper.

*   *   *

One summer afternoon I flew to New York to visit my mother, who was still living there after the death of my father. That particular flight I sat by chance next to the conductor of the chamber music society, who had a score laid out on his lap for the entire trip. He was a middle-aged paunchy guy a few years older than me, by no means the handsome young man I'd imagined when my lover told me he'd been the love of her life. By way of the forced intimacy of airline flights, we introduced ourselves—he told me he was a composer, on the way to see his publisher. I toyed with the thought of mentioning our mutual acquaintance. I imagined telling him he had a child he knew nothing about. With a few words I could change his life, and

36

I had no idea what effect that change would have on him. The guy seemed so content, reading his score. Just who did I think I was? So as the plane touched down, and we went our separate ways, I remained silent.

*   *   *

Standing in the doorway of his new room, two floors up, facing the Capitol, he asked the night clerk not to tell his wife what room he was in.

"Don't worry," he said, "I heard her over the phone."

"I'm a little worried she'll call the cops."

"Don't worry about that. They know me. And anyway they have other things to think about tonight—there's some guy with a gun running around the Capitol." And then he said, incredibly, "If you need a little smoke, I have some I could share."

*   *   *

Some years later I had begun to spend my summers up north, and only by chance did I learn one day that the conductor had been found dead of a heart attack in a parked car on the side of a downtown street. The coroner surmised that he had suddenly felt sick, driving to his Wednesday gig, and he'd pulled over to wait for the feeling to pass.

*   *   *

Alone in the new room, he rummaged through his suitcase. He had a single joint. It was by then well after midnight, and as he lit up he told himself, *Merry Christmas.* He stood looking out at the spotlit Capitol. He remembered the descriptions he'd read of Capitol Square the night before the Yankees arrived in 1865. Where the hotel now stood there'd been a building that housed the Confederate secret service. When the order to evacuate arrived that afternoon, they started burning all their files, right out there in the street. As darkness fell the sparks from the burning files rose into the night sky. Before they departed, the Confederate troops smashed all the barrels of liquor in the storehouses, so the mobs wouldn't get them, and lit off the stored ammunition so the Yankees

37

wouldn't get it, and the fires spread and by midnight the whole downtown was ablaze.

All that night, refugees from the burning buildings had huddled on the square, watching as their world went up in smoke.

This Year Ralph Sees

This year Ralph sees the fox squirrels moving in. Energetic and athletic, they leap from the high branches of one tree to another—oak to pine, pine to basswood, basswood to oak. Ralph's seen them chasing the gray squirrels, smaller and slower, from tree to tree. Bushy rust-red tail, two spots of lighter beige behind the ears, last winter there was only one: Ralph called him Rufus. This year they're here in crowds. There's even one Ralph's seen, tawny and well-fed, with a tail as blond as any movie star. That one he calls Blondie.

By spring they will be gone—but years from now Ralph will still see gray squirrels with small beige patches behind their ears, and on sunny days, red highlights playing in the fur along their backsides.

What We Can Learn from Other Primates

In the old days when I would visit my parents in the City, I sometimes left their apartment for a walk in Central Park, and one afternoon I dropped in on the Monkey House, though usually I despise such places. I stood there, watching aimlessly as two chimps in front of me sat on a trapeze, one preening himself, the other with a stare as vacant as my own. A man appeared beside me and began throwing pieces of bread over the barrier to the chimps. It fell through the top of the cage and the preening chimp kept reaching up and grabbing each piece as it fell through the bars. Chimps have long arms and this one's arm, from where he was sitting, could just about reach the top of the cage. A piece of bread got stuck there, and try as he might, twisting and stretching, the chimp couldn't reach it. Finally, frustrated, turning to one side, he hit his companion hard in the shoulder.

Muskrat

After the flood, Muskrat swam down and grabbed a clump of earth to bring back up to the surface—and from this Creator made Turtle Island.

A pile of rock had fallen, a year or two back, from the face of the limestone cliff, and from my canoe just offshore I see a muskrat sunning himself astride a slab, looking out over the water. When I get twenty yards or so away, he slips into the water. I figure he's gone for good until I drift a little further and see him floating on the other side of the rock. He's a young guy, by the looks of him, barely six inches long— and then his leathery tail. Finally he blinks and looks at me, then scrambles ashore and ambles off around the pile of rocks, sunlit drops of water in his fur. Moments later, a grayish brown bullet shape streaks under my canoe, disappearing into deeper water.

After the Reading

and fancies as delicate as arabesques of smoke
—Lafcadio Hearn

It wasn't that I wanted it to happen, he told me. We were sitting at a coffee shop downtown, and occasionally I'd see a bus pass by through the blinds half-drawn against the afternoon sun. He had called me, which was unusual, and said he wanted to talk. We used to play racquetball together, and since his surgery we had started meeting once or twice a week for coffee.

There wasn't much to tell, he said. She was a visiting poet, and his wife was away at her folks'. After the reading, they decided on an Irish bar, and he walked the several blocks in the mild air, and there were people sitting at tables on the sidewalk, and music from the door, and indoors the group of poets and some fiction writers, mostly students, a few professors. He didn't know any of the students and really only one of the professors, and then a few more people arrived and there she was, sitting across from him. It turned out she'd studied with an old friend who'd been his rival for their mentor's attention, and so they sat and talked, while all around them professors and students drank beer.

There was something about the way she held her body that moved him, though he couldn't say why, and when he looked at her face, in the dim light of the bar, it was as though her entire life was there—and his as well.

But he was married, he told himself: *She's leaving, and you're married.* He only half finished his beer . . . the room got hot and stuffy. By this time the music was reverberating around the bar, and the headache he'd had since the afternoon was growing worse. He told them all goodnight, and he walked out the door into the warm night of early May.

He told me he went home to give his dog her evening meds—and that's all that happened. She wanted nothing to do with him after that, ignoring his emails. He only sent her a few, he said, and then realized how crazy this all was.

The thing is, or was, he said, that as he left the bar, the full moon shining above the Capitol, a voice spoke in his head: *I want this woman to bear my child.* What am I to do with that, he asked—she nearly thirty years younger and he with a wife already?

The Clouds Pregnant with Rain

Shortly before the solstice, the catalpa at the other end of the block begins to flower. They start as small buds opening like tiny fists into white hands dripping fragrance into the air. For several days, walking the dog, I stop and raise myself on tiptoe to smell the flowers. Later, as they lie on the ground soggy and rotting, these blossoms stick to the bottom of my sandals.

The evening before I depart for the north country, I sit on the deck looking out at the lake. It's dusk, the leaves turning dark against the clouded sky. A cardinal lands in the cherry tree just in front of me, bright red in the fading air, not ten feet from where I'm sitting. He launches into his song—and repeats it twice before flying off into the trees. I hear his song once more from a distance, before it grows completely dark.

Two about Dogs

They say that the use of tools is peculiar to humans, and folks get all excited when a chimp uses a stick to get ants from where his or her fingers fear to go, or a crow uses a bit of fishing line to retrieve a piece of bait—but one afternoon when I took my dog for a walk, and after another long bout of chasing and retrieving a stick, when she dropped the stick to make angels in the snow, finally, stupid as I am—though quite good a throwing a stick—I noticed that she was, in fact, using the stick to scratch her back.

They say that one of the primary uses of language is to deceive, and this is one thing that humans do well, and I can't argue with that—but one evening we were sitting by the fireplace, and I got it in my mind to give the dogs a biscuit, or rather two biscuits, one for each dog; and the older dog ate hers in a hurry, and the younger dog kept his to savor, and was licking it in anticipation, when by the front door the older dog bristled and began to bark. As we live miles in the country, the hairs on the back of my neck twitched and the younger dog sprang up and raced barking for the door. The older dog broke off and retreated to the far side of the living room—where on the carpet lay a slightly-moistened, otherwise pristine, uneaten crunchy biscuit.

Pedestal

From out on the water, it looks to me like a duck sitting on a pedestal, asleep. A female mallard, speckled brown and white, atop a low brownish mound. Drifting closer in my canoe I see a bunch of little heads pressed close to her belly, a crowd of sleeping ducklings huddling up to her for warmth. They are all asleep, the little ones pressed against her, surrounding her, hiding the one leg she's perched on (the other tucked beneath her wing). One duckling opens his eyes, turns his head to look at me, neither of us moving.

Ralph Rises Early

Ralph rises uncharacteristically early and is out on the water in his canoe before the sun has gotten a hand-width off the horizon. When he reaches Towes Creek the sun is peering through the slight opening in the woods formed by the creek flowing nearly level into Sable Lake. The creek has formed a small delta of sand that extends into the lake, and tag alder have followed the expanding shoreline. There are dead limbs and branches sticking straight upward, leafless branches reaching into the air. Perhaps it's the angle of the sunlight or the early morning hour, but the combination of morning dew and sunlight reveals, in the bare branches of these tag alder, a myriad of glistening spider webs. Many of the trees have two or three webs in their topmost branches. Ralph stops paddling. He counts two dozen webs and then stops counting: the webs are like so many god's-eyes glittering in the branches of the tag alder.

On his way home, Ralph pauses at the bayou to listen to the bullfrogs advertising themselves to potential soulmates: *Here I am, come and get it, come and get it.* There are a few dead logs against the shore, gray and slime-covered, and Ralph sees a chipmunk run along one and pause there, perhaps wondering whether to traverse the log back to shore and then make his way around the bayou, through the swamp—or to cross the short stretch of water that lies between him and solid ground. This is not an entirely risk-free operation, since Ralph has seen, in the last day or two, a large turtle swimming in this part of the lake.

As Ralph watches, the chipmunk launches himself into the water, forelegs first like a swimmer starting a race, and swims, head above water, to the shore. He makes it safely across and clambers ashore onto a moss-covered log, where he proceeds to groom himself like a housecat.

Archive

You borrow her car and drive out of the city, a bright morning here south of the river, the trees already in full bloom and the fields beyond the pavement of the Interstate spreading away like summer. There's road construction and the day is turning hazy with a chance of showers in the afternoon. It's been raining off and on for weeks and already the rivers are rising.

After an hour you turn off the four-lane with the gray shapes of low hills ahead, take the state highway past the gas stations and eateries and strip malls, turn right off the frontage road by a park or cemetery, and then the road starts to dip and turn and you drive down a long green tunnel with the bluffs and leafy trees, over a bridge and into the town of Frankfort. Many one-way streets and old buildings and you have a hard time finding the archive, next to the old statehouse, and you have a moment of panic when a state worker, a woman leaving the building on her lunch hour, for it's noon already, tells you that you're in the wrong place and in any case, everyone has the afternoon off for Good Friday—though not, as it turns out, in the archive itself.

Later you wander the gift shop looking at pictures and books about Honest Abe, who Kentucky claims for its own, and pictures of horses in fields and wooden barns, and then you exit into a muggy oppressive afternoon with dark gray clouds in the western sky. It's the beginning of Easter weekend and the town seems deserted, shops closed up and only one or two cars on the street. You drive around, looking at the Federalist architecture with flowering trees all about, dogwood, cherry, redbud. Steep bluffs everywhere. The Kentucky River has cut its way downward over the years, and no glacier has come this far south to scrape the land overhead. You pause at "Celebrities Corner" to read the sign, names you recognize from the early years of Kentucky history . . . then drive by Justice Todd's large brick colonial.

Up the long highway out of town, past the Shoney's and the Ford dealer, and you're back on the highway to Louisville. Ahead the air is nearly black with snakes of lightning slipping between earth and sky, and then it starts to rain, a heavy tropical rain where you can barely see the taillights ahead, and in the gloom a heavier darkness slips by on the left—and then you're back on the city pavement and the rain has stopped and there is blue sky overhead. In the hotel room you turn on the Weather Channel and there are reports of a tornado in Shelbyville, just south of where you just passed by.

*   *   *

You leave the hotel and walks a few blocks south, the trees flowering along the streets of Old Louisville. It's Easter Sunday and here you are a Jew in a strange city, the neighborhood with its brick houses, no two alike and each one, it seems, larger than its neighbors, reminding you of somewhere you've been but you can't say exactly where that was.

It's Easter Sunday and the streets are mostly empty, occasionally a few cars in the lots across from one of the churches that seem to dot each street corner, but surprisingly little activity for the day that He arose. Two students (you surmise) pass you on the sidewalk still drunk from the night before: Hello, Sir, how'ya doin'? Halfway down the block you pass the Filson Historical Society mansion, now closed, where portraits of Kentucky colonels line the walls.

It's a humid morning. Across the street there's a squarish brick building broken up into apartments—you count six doorbells—that was once the home of your thrice-great-uncle who moved to Kentucky before the Civil War and made a fortune in bourbon and banking. For a year or two his niece—your great-grandmother—lived there after her mother died, a young girl but old enough to move out of the family home when there were too many mouths to feed, the life of a single father no easy thing after the war.

Across the street the porch is in disrepair, its Ionic columns eaten by rot. One window on the third floor of the house is boarded up, perhaps the room in which Martha made her home. It's on the south side, and there's a catalpa tree wedged in the space between the houses, rising above the roofline. On spring evenings, humid as this Easter Sunday, she sat beside the open window and smelled the catalpa flowers, their oh-so-sweet scent rising in the moist Kentucky air.

Like Our Shadow-Selves

It was the summer the Corps of Engineers were rebuilding the harbor breakwall, after a lapse of half a century, and the beavers were building a new lodge inland at Sable Lake. Each morning, if I arrived early enough, I'd see the male or sometimes the female with her yearling, nibbling small branches along the shore in the early morning light—but on days I was a little late, and they'd already, being nocturnal creatures, gone to bed, I'd take a closer look at the progress they'd made on their low mud-daubed hut.

Like our shadow-selves, they arise in the evening and live their lives at night, then slip off to sleep when we awaken. One morning I saw Mr. Beaver, the larger of the pair, swimming toward the lodge with a bunch of swamp-grass in his mouth, the tuft sweeping back over his head like some kind of weird camouflage or costume. King of the Beavers. He lay the grass against the hut, at the waterline, and dropped beneath the water toward the entrance, as it was dawn and time for sleep.

Toward the equinox they'd grown so used to my presence—it had been quite a while since I'd heard a tail-slap when I got too close—that for half an hour one morning, early postdawn with a chill wind blowing from the south, I sat in my canoe, some twenty feet from their lodge, while the two of them swam back and forth in front of me. The youngster was nowhere in sight, perhaps by that time having already left the family group. They swam in semi-circles, crossing alternately in front of the bow of my canoe, both of them looking at me all the while out of the one eye I could see beside their large noses.

I could see their heads clearly, their bodies blurred underwater: the male slightly larger than the female (about the same size as my ten-year-old border collie—but their noses flatter than hers). After a while the male turned toward the lodge, slipped with a slight *plop* beneath the surface of the water—and disappeared into a spot at the lodge entrance. And then I heard a brief sound like sloshing water, but there was no visible source. I imagined it was the sound, heard clearly through the thin walls of the lodge—once, twice—as the beaver shook himself dry.

The female then turned for home as well. At that moment a crow flew overhead slowly, looking down at us, cawing in approval or complaint. After a moment I heard another soft rushing, then out of the silence a sound of gnawing—perhaps a branch sticking into her back as she lay down to sleep. Gnawing again, then again silence . . . and only a single merganser shared the surface of the lake.

September

Last day of the summer, the sky clear after weeks of rain, a slight breeze tapers to calm. Late morning sun through the leaves, a pair of kingfishers arc from tree to tree along the shoreline, purple aster and joe-pye weed, mountain ash with its ripe red berries. In the bayou there's a single water lily, pure as any lotus-blossom, a couple of small flies feeding on its petals—then off to the side a splash, the kingfisher rises to a branch, minnow in its beak.

Whatever Dance

Whatever dance she was doing, it wasn't one I was familiar with. I kept stumbling over my own feet, or perhaps it was her feet, I was never too sure about that. Picture this: the river stretching out before you, lights of the city glittering off its surface—or maybe you're deep in the woods and the river is there before you, a presence in the night. Japanese lanterns on the black wrought-iron fence, the dance floor smooth beneath your feet (bare feet, no doubt, it being summer).

And the music? I couldn't tell you, after all this time. A waltz or two, a few sad sentimental tunes. You know the story: boy and girl, he off to the war and she along to college. A walk to the water's edge— and, bare feet, a splash in the current. As though it were yesterday, the smell of shampooed hair. Perhaps, for a moment or two, we got it right, the dance, our feet together, sliding on the sawdust floor. It's hard to say.

Crows

It was one of those rare afternoons when only slight riffles disturb the cloudless surface of the lake. Setting out in my canoe I saw perhaps a hundred crows settling in the maples which surround the bay, leaves yellow now in the October sun. By the time I returned, an hour later, the crows, so I thought, had dispersed, and only a few flew about in the trees as I paused, paddle lifted, feeling the sunshine on my face. I made a couple of tentative caws.

Suddenly the bright yellow leaves were filled with crows. They flew out from cover, crossing from one branch to another, all visible for a moment as they stared at me: black and gold, where before there had been only gold. Then they were gone, and once again only a couple of crows flew lazily about.

Turtle in the Afternoon

A month or so after the equinox—the lake empty, even the grebes have flown south already—I take my canoe out, one last time on the water before the autumn storms come sweeping in off Lake Superior with their promise of sleet and snow. The temperature is hovering around fifty with a slight south wind, the sun at mid-height through wispy cirrus clouds—and I paddle into the little bay where, two summers ago in the midst of heavy drought, the beavers built a new lodge. I haven't seen them since—perhaps they left for the backwoods when the swamps filled up again. The trees around the bay are mostly bare by now. There's an old birch that fell into the lake years back, and one large section of the trunk extends upward a foot or two above the water. As I paddle closer I see at eye level a turtle who has crawled up and out along a branch to catch the last warmth of the afternoon sun. He looks back at me—no fear—not scrambling off into the water as turtles usually do, but just sits there, head extended, looking right at me as I pause, mid-stroke, and watch him watching me.

A Black Spruce Meditation

Slowly the daylight fades. My dog and I sit looking out over the valley, until we can no longer see the clouds reflected in the river, the dark spruce angling toward the sky.

A Puffball Nearly Spherical

Now the solstice is just days away. Late morning sunlight slips through hazy clouds onto snow. In a few hours the sun will slide behind the hill while it's still mid-afternoon. Outside my study window there's a cardinal perching in the barren lilac. The bird's a puffball nearly spherical with winter down—a spot of bright red against the snowy hillside.

from *What the Raven Said*

Ralph in His Canoe

The sandpipers are back, bobbing up and down on nearly-submerged rocks by the shore, flying by Ralph (in his canoe) with their odd, downward-curving wings. The loons are all gone now from the lake, heading north for the summer. It's been raining this morning, a steady drizzle; a slight breeze ruffles the water. Up along the shoreline Ralph sees a single flowering crabtree, its blossoms like small explosions of light. In the water still lucid with spring Ralph catches a quick sight of a carp before it swims away, a murky shape longer than his forearm.

As Ralph rounds Second Point it stops raining, though the clouds remain. Soon Ralph finds himself in a flock of swallows swooping and weaving through a swarm of mayflies. Ralph has often seen these birds actually dip into the lake to catch their dinner, then shake themselves off and launch themselves upward in one motion—but today they never touch the water.

A cloud of swallows surrounds Ralph as he lifts his paddle and floats, motionless, upon the flat gray surface of the bay.

Ralph Goes to the Birds

It's the first hot day of the year, the trees a lime-green mist across the hills. Ralph's wife has left for the city and Ralph goes out to play guitar on the porch. An American plum is a splash of white on the hillside—the grass in the pasture is already green. By the porch the mountain ash has bare limbs through which Ralph can see the green hillside.

As Ralph sits playing it starts to rain—rain pours off the porch roof, rain in torrents bends the grass in the pasture. In a while the rain slows and stops, the sky clears, but Ralph keeps playing the same slow tune, trying to get it right.

The barn swallows soon appear with the sun to eat the spring's first crop of bugs—they flit in and out through the porch and Ralph's surprised at how close they come. Finally Ralph gets tired of playing, puts his guitar back in the case, and sits watching the sun on the lime-green hills and green fields, the puffy clouds of the first hot day of the year.

Suddenly two swallows are flying straight at Ralph. Abruptly they stop, hovering in front of him, twittering back and forth like teenagers in a school parking lot. Then just as suddenly they fly off, and as Ralph sits startled one of the swallows reappears, gliding by him to perch on a thick porch beam—and for a long moment the bird looks back at him.

In a Month This Will All Be

I followed my own trail here.
—Gary Snyder

Ralph comes down over the crest of the ridge, limestone outcroppings, the sun hot in May. Ralph's dog runs through the woods, a flash of black and white he can see through the small green leaves. In a month this will all be overgrown. Here's a small cave eroded back under the ridgetop, just large enough to crawl into out of the rain (though it's sunny today) and next to it an opening surrounded by fallen rock, just about large enough for a dog to lie down in.

Climbing around the thick oak that blocks the front of the cave, Ralph sees almost in the center of the circle of rocks a fragment of white bone, a leg bone perhaps of some small animal, finger-size, bleached white over the years—chewed on, Ralph sees, looking closer, picking it up, by several different sets of teeth.

He'd been walking down over the ridge into the valley, a warm spring day, and caught in a sudden thundershower, crawled in under the limestone to wait out the rain. His dog lay nearby in the rocks, chewing a bone he'd brought for her, as he dozed off to the sound of rain on the oak leaves—ten thousand years ago, yesterday.

The Naming of Muskrat Point

Early morning, and the water is flat, unruffled. In the shallows, spawning carp swirl and thrash. At times one raises himself nearly out of the water, muscles tense and glistening, the long fish arched in passion. Just down from where the cliffs run back into the hillside, there's flowering hawthorn, white flowers flowing to the water's edge like a bridal train.

From twenty-two miles above, a NASA photograph of Madison shows Lake Mendota, Picnic Point and Second Point clear as thumb and first finger of a giant's hand—and what's even clear on a close look is that Second Point isn't one, but two small promontories separated by a stretch of curving shoreline.

By a trick of morning sunlight, as I round the first of these small headlands—going east, facing open water—I'm invisible to a muskrat swimming up along the shoreline just the other side of a large rock. (Muskrats, I've noticed, seem quite nearsighted in the open air, though perhaps under water they are Deadeye Dicks.) At first I don't see this creature, but rather a bit of greenery—a sprig of basswood leaves, on closer look—moving along the shoreline. Immediately I stop paddling, and the muskrat, blinded perhaps by the glare of the low morning sun, continues to swim toward me. As I watch, drifting only slightly on the flat water, I see the animal turn and swim into a dark spot between two rocks just at the end of the promontory, perfectly hidden by a willow tree that's collapsed across the rocks into the water and is still leafing out. It's only by the slightest chance that I see the entrance to this muskrat den. (On future days I will confirm the comings and goings of the muskrats—two of them, I learn: one morning I see one enter the den with some young willow leaves and, moments later, a smaller one emerge.)

Every Day Ralph

Every day since his divorce was final, Ralph puts his canoe in the water. First he must take his canoe out of the cave-like "boathouse" the previous owner built out of limestone and mortar at the base of the cliff, just high enough for Ralph to stoop over in—a dirt floor usually moist and sometimes, when the lake is high, puddle-deep in water—and wide enough for a rowboat. Ralph has been told by a neighbor that the professor used to camp out here by the lake when his wife was mad (angry perhaps that her husband was spending such long hours in the laboratory, returning after dinner to check on his experiments, then coming back to the lake to spend the night amidst the rustling of the oaks, the bright stars over the water). Dank it is, the boathouse, though more than large enough for Ralph's canoe. Often he sees, in the bottom of his canoe, a daddy longlegs, or several, for a multitude thrive there in the damp confinement of the boathouse.

Today Ralph leaves the daddy longlegs undisturbed in the bottom of his canoe. For the story goes like this: Just a year ago, out on the water one evening to watch the sunset, Ralph is startled by the soft touch of insect feet on his face and reaches up to brush the thing away—and brushes as well his glasses, which falling through the water fade quickly before he can even think not to move lest he capsize—leaving him, this Fourth of July weekend, unable to drive north for his vacation. . . .

And so, in due fashion, awaiting his new glasses, Ralph is still around town when his wife returns from a business trip to Australia. For a week, recovering, as she says, from jet lag, she's awake at night wandering around the house while Ralph sleeps alone in their double bed, hearing the sounds of old Joni Mitchell songs drifting up from the living room. When he awakens in the morning she is asleep on the couch and the bottle of scotch stands nearly empty. Finally, the evening before he leaves to drive north, dinner on the table, the sun setting behind a mystical screen of oh-so-slightly-moving basswood leaves, she announces she's in love with another man.

Ralph, out in his canoe in the morning light of another season, feels gratitude to the daddy longlegs in the bottom of his canoe. Had he left on time for vacation, she would perhaps (as so often in the past) have buried the truth beneath a veneer of lies . . . and he might, so he thinks, still be married to her, and not have met the woman who's become his lover—(but that's another story).

So every day, since his divorce, Ralph puts his canoe in the water. In the morning light he takes the daddy longlegs for a ride. Together they glide on the wide flat lake, clouds and water, blue sky and sun. *Thank you, Brother Longlegs* . . . Ralph breathes steadily, his paddle moving in his hands.

The Night the Honey Locusts Bloom

Late one night at the beginning of June, the honey locusts at the end of Ralph's street begin to bloom. That night, walking his dog, when he turns the corner at the end of the block he's swept by a sweet exotic fragrance, delicate as the perfume his lover wears at bedtime. Back and forth Ralph walks to find the exact spot beneath the trees—at least a dozen, he's counted them—which blossom on the same evening (a sign, he has read, that the trees are a single clone). Ralph stands there with his dog, taking deep breaths through his nose, trying to prolong the sweet smell of the honey locusts. In a day or two, he knows, their dry flowers will fall—and lie alongside the street like the first snows of autumn.

Vacation Notes

1) Out on Lake Superior a fog bank rises in the purple distance. It's still cold here on the Point—lilacs blooming at the end of June.

2) A starling nests over the front door. First morning there's a dead one at my feet, it looks like a miniature ostrich—hairless, stomach bulging like a fried clam.

3) I won't ever see Lee Johnson again on the Old Seney Road. I used to pass him driving out to his camp somewhere on the Whitewash Plains, a wizened face through the window of his pick-up, nodding or smiling, just the two of us on the dirt road through the woods—you hardly ever pass anyone else out there, sometimes a lost tourist going too fast.

4) I buried my old dog's ashes up by the river on the high banks, next to a good-sized white pine on one side and on the other a huge old stump—high, in the breeze, overlooking the river.

5) I spent the day there, looking out over the water and the forest, and as night began to fall a single gull flew down the valley, toward me and by me—cruising—just overhead, and down along the river toward Lake Superior.

Ralph Attends the Turtle Convention

Just days before the solstice, Ralph enters the spring-fed bayou, his canoe slipping through a narrow opening in the marsh. A sun-hot morning, and the air is perfectly still here in the circle of water surrounded by trees. Wild iris are violet along the shore. Water lilies, white and yellow, dot the surface of the water.

Ralph hears the *chung chung* of bullfrogs all around him. Dragonflies zip back and forth across the pond. There are turtles of all sizes—two inches to half a foot across, he reckons—resting on the logs at the edge of the pond, watching him as he drifts upon the water. He stops counting when he reaches a baker's dozen. Three turtles, particularly wary, slip back into the water—but the rest continue to watch him. After a time, he oh-so-slowly turns the canoe and, not lifting his paddle from the water, starts back to Sable Lake. The turtles do not move.

The next day Ralph returns to the bayou, and the turtles are gone.

Lake Solstice

Today's the solstice: mountain ash along the shore lift their white flowerheads like candelabra. When I pass the mouth of Towes Creek, paddling steadily, an eagle flaps outward from the tallest spruce along the shoreline. As the eagle rounds the point ahead of me, a slight movement reveals a deer standing in the shallows. She looks upward for a moment as the eagle passes overhead, then slips back into the trees.

Eagle and Otter at Midsummer

—for Jim Harrison

It was the summer that fifty white pelicans appeared one Sunday morning just off Coast Guard Point, diving for whitefish as the fishermen strung out along the pier stopped what they were doing and gaped. The solstice was just days past, and there were hundred-knot winds in Minnesota that, presumably, blew the birds off their intended course to their summer home five hundred miles to the west of here.

Later that same day I went canoeing on Sable Lake and saw three eagles circling above me. I looked again a moment later and they were gone, too high for me to pick out against the bluest of skies. A fourth one stayed back in the crooked pine by the place I've begun to call Eagle Cove, so many times I've seen eagles there in one tree or another.

Now I've rounded the point and reach the spot, thick with wild iris, where I turn for home. I'm resting a moment or two, the paddle across my knees, absorbed by the silence of the evening, when I realize that for some time I've been hearing a *tsk tsk tsk* as though someone's trying to get my attention: *Hey, Bud, over here.* I turn and see an otter, head above the water, watching me. Then—having seen enough of this intruder—he drops back down and disappears beneath the surface of the lake

In the Sportsman

In the Sportsman Restaurant, old photos line the wall on either side of the huge brick fireplace—photos from the turn-of-the-century Grand Marais: old fishing boats, piles of raw lumber and white-pine boards, folks in dark suits and hats. Eating lunch in the cool dark bar, I see a crowd standing on the boardwalk in front of the old Hargrave & Hill general store, looking back across the dirt street at the photographer, who's standing pretty much where the soldier's monument is today. In the group of a dozen or so people, I see a dog that looks like my own—same size, same pattern of black and white, white paws, white muzzle, black ears and face and body. The dog watches the photographer across the street with his large portrait camera. My dog's standing there, what's most amazing, the same quizzical expression on her face—slightly sad, mortal, life all too short, looking across the street, in front of a store that nearly a century ago burned to the ground.

Ralph among the Lily Pads

Leaves all green and shiny screen the morning sun as Ralph sits in his canoe among the water lilies, and dragonflies scoot overhead.Suddenly a tadpole slithers onto a lily-pad, and stays: no gasping for air like a fish out of water, but he—or she—seems quite content looking upward at the sky. Ralph waits and watches and after a few minutes the tadpole squirms a bit and turns to face the other way, and one large eye looks back at Ralph like his puppy lying on the kitchen floor, head resting sideways on a paw as she looks upward to see if there's any food in the offing. Or perhaps the tadpole's looking at that blue sky, so different from the murky underwater view he's used to—this other world, so light and airy, around him.

Soon the tadpole shifts again, slips off the lily pad, and is gone.

What I Wanted to Tell You

Yesterday, walking on the high banks of the Sucker River, I saw a deer far below me with three fawns, standing on a mid-river sandbar. As I watched them, one of the fawns began to gambol and splash. Later I found the tiniest of toads, barely half an inch long. He had six pin-head spots on his back, rust-red like the pine needles he was sitting on. When I stood back up, a raven flew right overhead, circled around me several times, looking me over quite carefully. The bird was so close I could hear the sound of his wings through the air. The air was filled with late-summer light. All is well, the raven said, the world is fine.

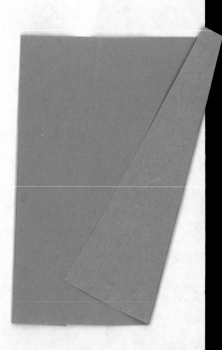

On the Last Day of Summer

On the last day of summer a raven did a barrel-roll in front of me. There I was in my canoe, paddling along—calm water in the cove, the September air still warm—when I heard croaking behind me, more drawn-out and extended than the usual guttural squawk that ravens speak with. Wondering what all the commotion was about, I looked up and saw a raven flying right above my head. Seconds later (and no more than a dozen feet in front of me), he tucked his wings in and rolled upside down, hanging for a moment in the air. I saw his feet sticking upward. Then, just before he began to drop, he righted himself and flew on.

I Bury My Mother's Ashes

A year before she died, my mother visited me in Grand Marais, and I brought her to the high banks of the Sucker River. It was late evening, and we walked the few dozen yards from where I parked the car to where I'm standing now, looking down at the river. We stood there as the air grew dark around us—and then looking upward we saw five sandhill cranes gliding low overhead, heading to their nests a half mile south of here, where the trees give way to the sandy Whitewash Plains.

I bury my mother's ashes up along the Sucker, in the same spot as my old dog, beneath a stout white pine. This tree was stunted early in life, but has grown out over the years and is now like the large flowering top of an ancient tree that's somehow been buried up to its neck in the sand of the high banks, so that its feet would be by the water's edge and my mother's ashes in the shade of its branches, looking out over the small river valley below.

Normally, there are few birds this late in the year, though today the air is mild. I've seen solitary ravens, and occasionally there's a nuthatch hidden in the pine, or a pair of chickadees. This day is different, however. Just as I step out to the overlook, a large red-tail hawk flies out from the top of the tall white pine down in the valley. At the same time two ravens fly across the valley squawking.

And this is just the beginning. After I place a small piece of granite over the pine needles that cover my mother's ashes, I begin to notice the birds. First a flock of cedar waxwings, gregarious as is their nature, follow me along the trail, so close I hear the rustling of their wings.

A flicker comes and sits on a branch not ten feet from me and, looking right at me, speaks to me in birdsong. I see many birds today I've never seen before and can't identify—which is not all that unusual, to be sure, though my mother would probably have known them all. As I stand looking out over the valley, another hawk drops out of a spruce and flies over the river. Since this hawk is actually below me, I can clearly see his reddish tail feathers.

And now a flock of crows flies into the valley. To be more accurate, they come in stages: first the advance scouts, who call back to their mates and alight on trees upstream. Then the others follow in waves, a few, a dozen, two dozen and more, cawing back and forth, settling for a while in the high branches of the pine and spruce, then continuing slowly southward until I can no longer see them. For a while longer I stand there, listening to their cries.

Only in Retrospect

It's only in retrospect that you can say, "This was the last warm day of the year"—sometime in early October, before the storm clouds come sweeping in across Lake Superior and the temperature drops twenty degrees in an hour. But yesterday was one such day, a mild wind blowing from the south, a few leaves dropping from the multi-colored trees.

More than a hundred crows flocked along the shore of Sable Lake, jawing back and forth into the morning air; two kingfishers flew upward into a cedar as I put my canoe into the water; out on the ruffled lake I saw a quintet of loons—flying south already?—and as I rounded the point near Towes Creek a bald eagle flew off from a maple and headed off down the lake. Though the crows were all about, they hardly seemed to notice: a few made cursory passes toward the eagle but almost, it seemed, pro forma, cawing in mild dismay—nothing, to be sure, like the way they mobbed an owl roosting outside my bedroom window one morning last winter.

In the afternoon I took my dog up to the Sucker River, and as we approached the high banks a single raven across the valley took off and circled overhead. By then the wind had died (only hours later it had shifted to the north and was building toward thirty knots), and we could hear the river gurgling like a broken faucet beneath us. Before us and around us and across the valley the trees stood motionless in their red and orange party clothes. Having worked all summer to store up food, and having been released till spring from the need to make a living, they were at last free to lose their green and stand for all to see in their true, most personal finery.

After another week or two and a few more north winds, the revelry would be over and they would strip down and go to bed naked, to sleep it off beneath the winter's snows.

Ralph Wakes One Morning

Ralph wakes one morning to the sound of Canada geese flying south. The window is open this misty September morning, a three inch gap beneath the shade, and in his green room at six a.m. the distant honking is unmistakable: a large flock, high in the sky, strung out in an uneven line heading southwest. Actually Ralph sees out of one eye the pillow and a bit of open window above the radiator. When Ralph sticks his foot out, the radiator is warm.

Soon Ralph has lifted his head from the pillow, he's gotten out of bed and gone to the back door to let the dog out. Ralph puts water on for coffee and goes to the front door to let the dog back in and get the paper. The enormous maple down the street is still mostly green but going yellow around the edges. The small maple in front of it is already entirely orange.

Dear Martha, Ralph writes, sitting at his desk later with the light from the rainy September day casting itself softly over the yellow pad, *It's getting to be fall here and the trees down the street are already turning, we had such a cold summer and now as much rain as you must be getting on the West Coast. . . .*

Ralph remembers flying over the Sierras that April and seeing out the window of the jet the full moon shining down on the snow-covered mountains. When he got to the San Francisco airport she was waiting for him, blue eyes the color of chicory and a purple leotard under her white shirt. He thought about going out the door with her and making love right there in the camper in the airport parking lot, as they swayed together and he smelled through her blond hair frangipani.

It took over three hours to get to the low mountain by the Russian River—the old Ford would hardly go fifty—back to her small house in the redwoods, a large wine vat someone had covered with a Plexiglas roof. The full moon shone through the enormous trees. They left the car by the side of the dirt road, walking the last hundred yards through a dew-soaked meadow. The chill of the night air settled on them. Ralph had been traveling all day.

By evening it has stopped raining and Ralph hears a squeak or two beyond the open window by his desk. He has been writing all day, one thing or another, proposals, critiques, correspondence—but his letter remains unfinished. Ralph notices that the bird feeder is empty, since the sparrows and chickadees have been feeding all morning and afternoon. Even in the rain they show up to eat and gossip. But the cardinal only comes at dusk, often when the feeder is empty, and though Ralph now goes out to fill it, the cardinal's a cautious bird and flies off when Ralph opens the back door.

When Ralph gets back to his desk he sees the cardinal has returned to the feeder. She's sitting there eating, looking up as she chews her sunflower seeds to watch the door and Ralph's window. Ralph hears in the quiet September evening the distinct sound of the cardinal cracking sunflower seeds. Slowly the air darkens. Soon, Ralph is sure, the single cricket in the catalpa out back will start his end-of-summer song.

Old Possum

The only marsupial in North America. Five toes on each foot; inside toe on hind foot opposable (an aid in climbing) and without claw. . . . Among the most primitive of living mammals. . . . May live seven years or more.
—*Mammals* (Peterson Field Guides)

Here's how it happens. The night before the full moon (the air still mild in October), while Ralph is walking his dog and the moon's shadows play under the oaks, he sees up the block, beneath the sole streetlight, just as his dog comes alert, an animal about the size of a large cat, with a pointed nose—and then it's gone and Ralph's dog is whining and straining at the leash.

The next morning, from his canoe out on the water, Ralph sees a possum by the shore, standing on a rock, face pointed downward. As Ralph moves closer, he sees that the creature's head is nodding like an old man falling asleep in his chair. When his nostrils hit the water, small bubbles appear on the lake's surface and the possum jerks his head up. As Ralph moves even closer, the animal senses his presence and raises his head, and Ralph sees that he's blind, no eyes left in his sockets, and yet he seems to have a clear idea of just where Ralph is, and starts to back up, the prehensile thumbs on his rear feet gripping the slick rock, appearing to Ralph as worn and lumpy as his father's hands before he died.

Later that day, walking his dog, Ralph sees that the possum has lain down in the water and is curled up with his head on a small rock and the gentle waves lapping his fur. At first Ralph thinks he's dead, but once again the creature must sense Ralph's presence—or smells his dog—and slowly he gets to his feet and faces them. Ralph withdraws, keeping his dog close by him on the leash, and the possum lies back down. A late bloom of algae by the water's edge covers the lower half of the possum in a pale green.

That night the full moon spreads its quicksilver across the lake, and the air is still mild. The next day, when Ralph walks his dog, the wind is blowing out of the northwest and there's a chill in the air. When Ralph gets to the lake's edge, he sees the rocks are empty. In the night,

Ralph imagines, beneath the soft canopy of the full moon, the possum rose like Elijah and, crossing the light-filled lake, ascended heavenward . . . while the autumn moon, a perfect circle of white, moved through the cloudless sky.

Mosquito Bay

The wind, the horn, the gulls: another rainy day on the Point. It's autumn now as I write, yellow leaves slipping by the window, these days growing shorter.

*   *   *

Tonight the wind has stopped. Out here on Coast Guard Point, a sandy spit of land sticking into the cold blue of Lake Superior—and creating a harbor of refuge midway between Marquette and the Soo (in the last century and a half, many ships have gone down along this windy coast, attempting to make Mosquito Bay in a storm)—out here nothing grows but Balm-of-Gilead, on this sandy soil, really no soil at all, just sand. The large trees rustle in the slightest breeze, and the wind seems never to stop, constant, blowing off the lake (or rarely from the south: always, in that case, it seems, heavy with moisture—when there's a warm wind blowing across the bay, you can smell the damp pine forests).

Usually the wind is constant . . . but not tonight. When I wake, abruptly, I hear the silence. I put on a heavy wool shirt and go out on the porch. The leaves are still. Hours ago the moon has set, and the stars are brilliant above the dark water. Now I can hear the surf—waves rolling in from the northwest to crash on the sandy beach of East Bay. I stand on the porch overlooking the water and watch the northern lights pulsate across the sky "like God's own orgasm."

*   *   *

If you head north from Chicago, Mosquito Bay is about as far as you can get without crossing Lake Superior. Only a couple of hundred people live there, year round. It's one of the few places left in the U.S. where you can still call someone using only the last three digits of her phone number.

Empty stretches of café-au-lait sand beach surround the protected harbor, gulls turning above the water, spots of white against the spruce-and-pine forests. If it were any warmer, any other climate or location, a beach this white and sweeping would be jammed with bodies,

83

the bay ringed with houses instead of dark forests that have trouble remembering the sun. Both Marquette and the Soo are more than a hundred miles away.

Red pine forests, ghosts of sunlight on the dune grass, the cry of the seagulls like children at play. Bleached drift-logs lie on the beach, torn from Lonesome Point in a November gale. All last night there was lightning but no rain—this morning, fog: you couldn't even see across the bay. Every fifteen seconds the foghorn sounds, a low bass note that echoes off the escarpment back of town.

*   *   *

It's getting to be winter. One morning the bay is freezing, ice floating near the shore, even the gulls are gone. Silence. (Only a couple of crows and some sparrows are left from all the birds singing in June: the geese, the chorus of mourning doves, the woodcock at dawn.)

What the Raven Said

Once there were wolves in the forest—and then the white folks came and cut the great pine for their homes in the city, and a wolf or moose these days is a rare sight in the scrubby brush that covers the sand. Only blackened stumps remain of the huge trees, "lighter-wood" that'll burn and burn in your campfire. And the river itself, the white men changed its path with dynamite and steam. They swerved it to empty twenty miles west, into the bay where their mills and steamers waited for wood—and now spoonful by spoonful, sand from the Whitewash Plains fills the white folks' harbor.

Paddler's Technique

Apart from the risk of drowning, hypothermia can
quickly cause death to capsized canoeists . . . whenever
the water temperature added to the air temperature
gives a number lower than one hundred.
                        —*Guide to Canoeing*
                        (Wenonah Canoe Co.)

Ralph knows it's getting time to quit when he returns home one morning
and the tip of the third finger of his left hand (that is, the third finger
of his wetsuit glove, which covers a polypropylene liner, which covers
his warm flesh) is covered with ice. Perhaps he should have known
when he set out, since the air, though calm, was well below freezing,
and Ralph had to break a thin layer of ice away from the shore before
paddling. The water seems viscous at this temperature, like vodka left
in a freezer, hard to push about with a paddle, hard to move through
in a boat. The few miles that normally take Ralph an hour today take
him nearly two.

So Ralph knows for sure it's time to quit when he gets back
home and finds the tip of his finger encased in ice. Apparently this is
all that touches the water (as he was taught, so many summer ago, that
his fingers should just "kiss the water"), and, like a candle hand-dipped
in tallow, each time Ralph slips his paddle through the water and lifts it
back into the freezing air, another thin layer on his finger turns to ice—
so that Ralph's third finger of his black neoprene wetsuit glove has a
hard clear teardrop-shaped fingertip . . . which now, in the warmth of
Ralph's mudroom, is slowly melting.

Now the Lake Is Empty

Now the lake is empty. The last ducks have left. Skinning the water's surface, so clear you can see the sandy lake bottom beneath it, is a thin green layer of ice. In this looking-glass you can see reflected the puffy white clouds motionless in the blue sky, like the depths of a lake you've never seen before. Here, at last, is a world you can learn to call your own.

from *White Pine Sucker River*

Where Ralph Lived

The upstairs of my house is a remodeled attic. Perhaps forty years ago they plastered the slanted ceiling and painted the walls a dull green, perhaps it was a bright green at the time but it's faded over the years and now it's a dull light green. The floors are painted brown. The walls on the third floor of the house I grew up in were painted the same green, but what's even more remarkable is that my attic these days smells the same as that other attic, perhaps it's the smell of old plaster. It makes me think of rainy afternoons with model trains whizzing back and forth across the dull green room.

These early spring mornings I often walk the dog the few blocks down to pick up the newspaper, then home along the Chicago & NorthWestern railroad tracks. It's often cloudy, in April, and the wind is still cold and my dog, a border collie whose ten years have only slightly moderated her energy, runs up and back across the backyards. We walk home by the Theo. Kupfer Iron Works, the Morris Heifetz Salvage truck out back with its hand-painted motto, "Scrap is Forever." Down the tracks, beyond a gravel loading yard the Garver's Supply Co. warehouse is like a Charles Sheeler painting, all light and surfaces, the faded white words, the gray superstructure of the grain elevator rising toward the clouds.

At the Party

Ralph has just bought himself a new pair of red sneakers. The catalpa tree beyond his porch has fragrant trumpet-shaped flowers among the huge leaves. When Ralph looks closely at the catalpa flowers he sees on the pale blooms red streaks the same color as his new sneakers.

Across the street, spring pigeons call each other names. She sat there, the window was open and the surf of traffic mixed with the warm air.

Saturday night, at the party, Fred asks him, Why red? They were on sale, says Ralph, the only ones left. When Ralph gets home the night-air is still warm and, falling asleep, he can smell the catalpa flowers.

From Where He Sat

From where he sat Ralph could see the top of the University buildings peeking over the crest of his neighbor's elms. They were elms, weren't they? What the hell, he'd been over it in his mind several times and they were definitely elms. . . .

From the next room, Martha: Elms, dear? Did you say elms?

No question about it, they were elms.

He wrote: "This street is silent. Outside my window a silver maple drops yellow leaves onto weeds and bricks."

*   *   *

It was Sunday afternoon and in the next room the T.V. with the football game he'd just turned off. Outside the windows his neighbor's elms were yellow already, leaves streaming in the wind off the lake. Angela had been born in Port Washington, her parents Republicans, her mother selling real estate back in the sixties—and perhaps a church project or two when Angela used to sneak off to Milwaukee and hang out in the Public Museum.

Once a week he would walk up to class and spend a couple of hours looking at Angela's pre-Raphaelite face across the table, the windows growing dark outside the concrete building . . . that Yeats poem, he'd slip it into her mailbox someday.

In the hallway she had touched him once: "I don't date married men, generally speaking." She was writing a paper on Sylvia Beach.

*   *   *

He remembered his father walking the halls of the hospital, tinsel still on the Christmas tree, telling a joke he'd heard first when he reached puberty, twenty years earlier. "I don't generally but you talked me into it," after "I'm a man of few words, do you or don't you?"

In the autumn wind, yellow leaves, a hint of rain . . . and she touched him in the hallway, beyond the windows the skyline and the lake.

Fall and he'd sit on the back porch—or was it the front porch, he'd never really been sure—looking off across the fields at the telephone poles he liked to exercise his eyes by focusing on . . . the gravel of the driveway, year by year, becoming thicker with weeds.

*   *   *

And Angela. Walking beneath the yellow leaves: "We moved to Port Washington when I was fourteen. We used to walk out on the breakwater in the middle of the summer for the cool breeze. My father worked for the power company and at Christmas we always baked almond cookies."

When he'd gotten back to the farm at the end of summer, he'd sit out on the porch in the September darkness. Frank was living out there then and they'd go together to do the laundry down in Sauk City, eat dinner at the Penguin. Now he'd cut his hair and was working for a computer company. "The long evenings out on the river in the canoe, just me and Frank watching the Great Blue Heron."

They went out to visit the place. He remembered the phone call in the night—he thought it was his father at first then remembered his father had died six months before—"The farm burned to the ground last night, no one hurt but I lost everything but my guitar." It was October by then and the trees . . . the oaks russet, the wind through the dead and dying leaves of the cottonwood. There was a big hole in the ground that used to be the basement where he stored the books one summer when he and Martha had gone out west and Frank's waterbed had leaked and he'd lost the first edition of Yeats and the Byron his great-grandmother had carried from Brooklyn to St. Louis. There were trees growing out of the basement.

*   *   *

Now in the October wind the leaves blew and from the next room, Martha: Elms, dear, did you say elms? By now it was a joke, the two of them walking along the beach, and barely heard over the roar of the surf, "Elms, dear. Did you say elms."

Angela, was that really her name . . . what had Donna said at the party, Are you two going to jump into bed or what. Or what, I guess.

"I used to have a first edition of Yeats but the waterbed leaked . . . not mine, but what can you do."

Beyond the window there was the shadow of the porch and beyond the backyard some trees. From where Ralph sat he could see the trees and, beyond them, some concrete. Martha in the next room moving back and forth: The elms, don't forget the elms. "The basement, he could see the basement now naked in the afternoon. Gray clouds over the hill."

White Pine Sucker River

Ralph takes a walk with his dog. It's late August, an afternoon of bright warm sun, at least away from Lake Superior where the wind blows straight off the cold waves. Yesterday Ralph watched that wind at work moving the great dunes along, throwing sand back over the spruce all along the top of the cliffs.

Yesterday they went walking down from the dunes, looking out through spruce and mountain ash (still green with bright red berries) at the waves and white foam advancing before the northwest wind. When they come out onto the beach the wind whips sand into their eyes.

Ralph's dog stands, back turned to the wind, watching the cliff: as the wind loosens sand and carries it over the dunes, rocks the size of golfballs and baseballs come rolling down, first one, close by, then another, twenty yards off, then another, closer, in the other direction. Ralph's dog, surprised, jumps back as a rock the size of a large orange comes splashing through a pool left by the waves. And all the while waves crash and roll the rocks on the beach, grinding them into the sand their ancestors have long since become.

But today Ralph and his dog have walked back into the woods. It's quiet here, away from the lake. And soon Ralph realizes that mostly, along the lake's edge, he's seen red pine and spruce . . . but here they've been walking through a large stand of white pine. Ralph and his dog soon come to where the Sucker River crosses the trail. The river has cut through the dunes here on the way to the lake, and Ralph walks up to the lip of the cut, looking down over roots and overhang, down the steep sandy slope to the stream. He swings over the edge and leaps down the sand, enormous strides taking him in seconds to the water. His dog whines and runs along the edge of the cut until she finds a spot slightly less steep and launches herself over the edge and down the shifting sand.

Here at the bottom the water runs over sand and fallen branches. Ralph sits by the stream and raises his face into the sun. Ralph opens his eyes. Years have fallen away. He sees down the cut an enormous white pine standing just beneath the sun. Its branches hang wide over empty space.

The white pine is huge, centuries old. One day, Ralph thinks, the sand will fall away from the roots just one handful too much and the pine will topple into the Sucker River. But now, with the sun hot on his face, Ralph sits on the grass and sand of the stream's edge. When he looks again Ralph sees way up along the edge of the cut his dog walking back toward him. She must be impatient, Ralph thinks. He gets up stiffly and climbs up the bank to meet her.

Weekend

All weekend long it rained and the wind blew leaves and walnuts out of the tree in Ralph's backyard. There was occasional lightning and Ralph heard the booming of walnuts on the roof as rather benign artillery, though he wouldn't want one to hit him on the head.

On Monday the rain had stopped and Ralph woke to the sound of geese squawking up beneath the still-solid clouds. The walnuts were mostly gone from the tree (for another two years), the leaves also, the bare branches looking already in mid-September like they would in the middle of winter. Walnuts lay across the lawn like small green baseballs . . . over a hundred, Ralph figured, on his small patch of backyard. All day long Ralph looks out his window to see the squirrel so flushed with food he's doing acrobatics on the hammock. He leaps from the tree, runs, stops, jumps up to the hammock, holds on for a few seconds, then flips in the air, once, twice, again . . . and jumps back to the tree.

At dusk, when light is barely light, one of Ralph's cardinals comes to feed at the feeder just beyond his window. Ralph has come to think of the birds as his, he supposes it's the same pair he sees, always this time of year by themselves. In the spring Ralph noticed how, holding a single seed in their beaks, they would give each other sunflower seeds. But now they come alone, and the quiet sounds Ralph hears like squeaks while they peck at the sunflower seeds are, he would like to imagine, for him.

Mickey

For a week or two he was having everyone call him Mickey. At first he just said, If you'd see the movie you'd understand, and pretty soon everyone had seen the movie and then he went back to being Morty. That was winter. We were meeting then a couple of times a week in the morning at the JCC to play racquetball. Mornings were the only time you could get a court, besides it was cheaper too. Morty was working second shift at the hospital, and I had Tuesdays and Thursdays off.

In the shower he would tell me about the drugs he mixed up for the terminal patients. Morty was a pharmacist, the end of a long road from the Bronx and a spell pig farming in Mt. Horeb. Then he got asthma from the pigs, no wonder, what's a nice Jewish kid from the Bronx doing raising pigs for Christ's sake? He'd bring his inhaler with him onto the court. My strategy therefore—he was also a bit overweight, a swimmer who years ago had stopped competing—was to get him running back and forth. I got a kick out of hearing him wheeze. No doubt because, a better player by far, he usually beat the shit out of me.

That winter was no fun anyway. The wind comes off the frozen lake in Milwaukee, from the pool of the JCC you can see through the misted wall of windows—what the hell's it cost to heat that place I wonder—a white expanse of ice snow and cloud. Sweating in my long underwear, I'd walk with Morty in the biting wind to get breakfast at the nearby Mafia hotel. I'd been bullied once in the restaurant there when I complained about the dessert, but I figured they wouldn't recognize me in the coffee shop.

By the time spring came, a month or two later, Morty was thinking about moving to Toronto, and Tuesdays and Thursdays I had started sleeping in.

Library

We might have given birth to a butterfly
With the daily news
Printed in blood on its wings

—Mina Loy

You've been in the Library now for hours. You came back after dinner and now you've fallen asleep. As a matter of fact it's so late that everyone else has left the library, but since you're tucked away in a corner by the window no one noticed you before they turned off the lights. It's April now and the moon is almost full and the clouds are scudding across the moon so it looks like the moon itself is moving quickly . . . and off to the east the Lake Michigan is dark, though even if you were awake you couldn't see the lake from here, where you're sitting by the window— or more factually, slumped over with your head back and your mouth open as though you'd fallen asleep on a plane. Books, several of them, are open in front of you.

On December 10, 1929, Harry Crosby, 31, and Josephine Rotch Bigelow, 22, were found dead together in a friend's apartment. They'd been lovers for a year and a half, though each was married to someone else. The *New York Times* the next day had this to say:

> The couple had died in what Dr. Charles Morris, Medical Examiner, described as a suicide compact. The police believe that Crosby, in whose hand they found a .25 [caliber] Belgian automatic pistol, had shot Mrs. Bigelow and then turned the weapon on himself. There were no notes and the authorities were unable to obtain information pointing to a motive for the deaths.[1]

In the dark library, in the overstuffed library chair, with the moon asserting itself through the windows your sleep is getting restless. It's almost, with the moon and the dark library, as though you're not asleep at all. It's as though you're hearing voices from far off, as if you're walking in a fog down a city street and there are people talking all around you but you can only see the glow of street lights and dark trees formless around you . . . and then suddenly faces appear out of the fog. This has all happened before, as a matter of fact you've been troubled with these dreams for months, but they've never been this vivid. The faces circle you, indistinct in the fog, and for the first time you can hear what they're saying . . .

Caresse Crosby: The lazy towers of Notre Dame were framed between the curtains of our bedroom windows.[2]

Harry Crosby: "I like my body when it is with your body. It is so quite new a thing."[3]

Stephen Crosby: The idea of your writing poetry as a life work is a joke and makes everybody laugh.[4]

Caresse: There was a swimming pool on the stream side of the courtyard, around whose paved shores coffee and croissants were served on summer mornings from sunrise until noon.[5]

Harry: The shattered hull of a rowboat stuck in the sand, a fire of driftwood, a bottle of black wine, black beetles, the weird cry of seagulls lost in the fog, the sound of the tide creeping in over the wet sands, the tombstone in the eel-grass behind the dunes.[6]

Hart Crane: Dinners, soirées, poets, erratic millionaires, painters, translations, lobsters, absinthe, music, promenades, oysters, sherry, aspirin, pictures, Sapphic heiresses, editors, books, sailors.[7]

Harry: What is it I want? Who is it I want to sleep with?[8]

Josephine Rotch: Do not be depressed. Take the next boat. You know I love you and want you.[9]

It's hard to believe you're still asleep, slouched over in the musty library chair. The moon is still poking through the clouds. If your eyes

101

were open you'd see moonlight across the books in front of you. But you're still asleep, cramped and uncomfortable as it must be. Perhaps you'll ache tomorrow. Outside the window the trees are dark in the shadow of the library. The faces turned towards you in the fog are indistinct—a crowd of strangers who seem, unaccountably, familiar. Like the time you met her at that party, from across the room and all the noise you thought to yourself, Where have I seen her before?—knowing that you   probably never had. And in bed the first time together, her dark eyes looking at you: Who is this woman? Yes, in the dark library, in the moonlight and the fog, you can hear the voices . . . what is it they're saying, what is it?

Archibald MacLeish: My impression was that it was all good fun, good decor, but not to be taken seriously. My own conviction was that he wasn't serious about it, till I found out the hard way that he was deadly serious about it.[10]

Harry: When I got home a riot with Caresse and she started to jump out the window got halfway over the balcony rail. It happened so quickly that I hardly had time to be frightened but now three hours later I am really frightened I hope I don't dream about it.[11]

Josephine: I love you I love you I love you.[12]

Harry: It was madness, like cats in the night which howl, no longer knowing whether they are on earth or in hell or in paradise.[13]

Josephine: Death is *our* marriage.[14]

MacLeish: As I sat there looking at his corpse, seating myself where I wouldn't have to see the horrible hole in back of his ear, I kept saying to him: you poor, damned, dumb bastard.[15]

You're awake suddenly in the dark library. The lights from Sonny's across the street are out, it must be after four. The moon is gone. You feel like shit. Time to walk the couple of blocks home in the April darkness . . . and the birds maybe already awake. You open the library door,

102

the air's a bit chilly. There's nothing like the taste of last night's coffee, you mumble to yourself and whoever else might be listening.

[1] *The New York Times*, December 11, 1929, quoted by Malcolm Lowry, *Exile's Return: A Literary Odyssey of the 1920s* (1934; rev. ed. New York: Viking Press, 1951), 282.

[2] Caresse Crosby, *The Passionate Years* (New York: The Dial Press, 1953), 105.

[3] E. E. Cummings, as (mis)quoted by Harry Crosby, *Shadows of the Sun: The Diaries of Harry Crosby*, ed. Edward Germain (Santa Barbara: Black Sparrow Press, 1977), 219.

[4] Stephen Crosby, letter to his son, quoted by Harry Crosby, *Shadows of the Sun*, 58.

[5] Caresse Crosby, *The Passionate Years*, 244.

[6] Harry Crosby, "The End of Europe," *transition* 16-17 (June 1929), 119; reprint, *Torchbearer* (Paris: Black Sun Press, 1931), 26.

[7] Hart Crane, postcard to Samuel Loveman, *The Letters of Hart Crane, 1916-1932*, ed. Brom Weber (New York: Hermitage House, 1952), 333.

[8] Harry Crosby, *Shadows of the Sun*, 256.

[9] Josephine Rotch, telegram to Harry Crosby, quoted by Geoffrey Wolff, *Black Sun: The Brief Transit and Violent Eclipse of Harry Crosby* (New York: Random House, 1976), 209.

[10] Archibald MacLeish, quoted by Geoffrey Wolff, *Black Sun*, 312.

[11] Harry Crosby, *Shadows of the Sun*, 277.

[12] Josephine Rotch Bigelow, telegram to Harry Crosby, quoted by Geoffrey Wolff, *Black Sun*, 285.

[13] Harry Crosby, unpublished notebook, quoted by Geoffrey Wolff, *Black Sun*, 283.

[14] Josephine Rotch Bigelow, letter to Harry Crosby, quoted by Geoffrey Wolff, *Black Sun*, 285.

[15] Archibald MacLeish, quoted by Geoffrey Wolff, *Black Sun*, 288–289.

Was It Louis Aragon

"Was it Louis Aragon who wrote that poem about how there's a moment at the center of a person's life that should be of the utmost significance, exactly half one's life gone by, but that it passes unnoticed a day like any other, dogs barking in the street, newspapers blowing in the afternoon breeze?"

"I'm sure I wouldn't know, dear," she said, wandering among the rocks at the water's edge. The small waves came up the beach and wet her tennis sneakers but she didn't seem to mind, looking intently in the growing darkness at the stones along the beach.

They'd driven off the highway into this cove of redwoods, not to see the sunset since the sun had already slipped into the fog. They'd stopped because they were tired of driving the old Pinto along the coast highway, brakes nearly gone, pumping them up for each hairpin turn. It was already dark here among the mystical trees—so he still thought of them, having just arrived in California. Nearly a decade ago now he'd first seen her working at the bakery, so struck by the blueness and clarity of her eyes that he'd bought a loaf of bread and run out the door immediately, driven all the way back to the farmhouse in a shivering fit.

He was walking by the creek that split the cove in two. The water ran over sand and rocks and he heard rather than saw it. She had come up behind him in the dark and was rubbing his shoulders. Her breath was on his neck, warm and regular. "Who was Louis Aragon anyway?" she asked. "That friend of yours in Boston you went to high school with?"

A Joe Pass Guitar Solo

I've fallen asleep in the afternoon. It's November and the radio is playing a jazz program from the local Public Radio station. But my father and I are in Fenway Park. It's June and the outfield grass is dark green (darker than the huge green left-field wall) and my father has just bought one of those ten-cent paper bags of peanuts (it must be close to a full pound of peanuts for a dime). We're both eating peanuts. My father's hands—which seem huge to me, the backs covered with veins "like a roadmap" as he used to say—are deft as hell with the peanuts: Crack and he tosses them into his mouth, the shells drop through the green slats of the seat.

It's the eighth inning and the Red Sox are behind by five runs. Ted Williams is batting and my father points out to me how perfect his swing is. "Look at that bastard swing," my father says—level as Nebraska." I don't think my father was ever in Nebraska. "But remember, Rob," he says, "he only hit .400 in his really good years. . . . Even at his best Ted Williams missed the ball six times out of ten."

It's getting to the end of my dream. I'm in that funny place where you're dreaming but you're also aware of the room around you. There's late-afternoon sunlight through the plants in my window and it sounds like Joe Pass on the radio, bass and piano comping in the background. Joe Pass's left hand is going all over the fingerboard of his arch-top Gibson and his right hand is in perfect time. The notes are like tropical birds flying from the small speaker of my radio . . . and suddenly all these bright yellow and blue and orange birds come circling and wheeling into Fenway Park. My father and I look up amazed at the bird-filled June sky.

One of the Guys

Sam's one of the guys around the office who's into baseball, you know the type, always going around talking about a trade or someone's injury or ERA. Sam's from Detroit. He grew up with other middle-class kids taking cars apart on weekends and going to Tiger Stadium. There wasn't much else to do because the girls in those days liked the older guys who were already in college. So Sam watched the Tigers and completely restored, piece after piece, the 1931 "Tudor" Model A his grandfather bought for fifty bucks in 1950. When Sam finished it the three coats of black enamel shone in the fluorescent light of his father's garage.

Sam's getting fat going through his thirties. We used to play racquetball together but then I discovered religion and Sam started taking care of the kid he and his wife conceived after a Grateful Dead concert. His red hair is, these days, cut pretty short.

So one afternoon at work Sam came up with his Al Kaline idea. There he'd stand, number 6 in his old Tiger uniform, looking not a day over forty-five. He'd be holding up a package of alkaline batteries: "Al-Kaline batteries, hit harder, longer!" Not bad, eh? Sam says over coffee. He batted .297 lifetime, you know . . . and it was only in the last two weeks of his last season that he slipped below .300.

Every Night He'd See Her

Every night he'd see her on the news—she did the weather. It had been six months now since she'd moved out and she'd gone through the whole range of temperatures, starting with a stretch in the nineties when he got back last summer—the avocado, one of them at least, was already dead by then, dropping all its leaves in the heat, so she told him, having kept his plants watered while he was away. And now the temperature dropped regularly below zero at night—she still did the weather, her breasts almost visible—but could she know he was watching, some impossible refraction of the TV screen, photons rushing backward. . . .

He still saw her occasionally, their carts bumping in the grocery aisle, by the frozen food perhaps, their hands touching reaching for the orange juice. He turned away at the last minute, before she saw him, turning again as he remembered he needed coffee. He'd started falling asleep right after he ate dinner and waking up late in the evening, his downstairs neighbors had by then already gone to bed—and only once did he hear them making love, tenuous sounds he heard since he was listening. Now late at night he'd make himself a cup of coffee and listen to an all-news radio station from Chicago. This seemed to loosen him up and he could stay awake for hours waiting for the final scores of west coast ballgames.

Finding Token Creek

Before the Yahara enters Lake Mendota, it widens out and flows through Cherokee Marsh. The marsh surrounds a fairly wide river there, in some places nearly a hundred yards from shore to shore. From a canoe on the water there are of course some houses visible, but often it appears that you're paddling out in the wilderness, blue water and sky surrounding you, green trees and marsh-grass, low hills down where the river flows into the marsh. Along the shore are reeds and cattails, pickerelweed with its large arrowhead leaves, wild bergamot.

Yesterday was one of the last true spring days around here before summer comes along and fills the air with moisture, the sun too hot at midday to stay out in for the two or three hours it takes to paddle to the river at the head of the marsh from the gravel parking lot down at the end of the dirt road that School Street becomes if you follow it long enough, way off behind the shed where the highway department stores its winter plows. The marsh is protected, no cars allowed for its entire length—and that's why from out on the water few houses are visible. The wide buffer of marsh between the river and subdivisions is nearly impenetrable this late in June, with blackberry patches poison ivy and interwoven willows and oaks.

Yesterday the wind was blowing from the northeast. The wind very rarely blows from the northeast around here, only when there's a strong weather system sitting right over Hudson Bay, turning the air down upon us after it passes over the 35-degree water of lake Superior three hundred or so miles to the north. This makes it especially a pleasure to be out paddling around—my dog sitting in front of me in the bow— since it means that returning I won't have to fight the prevailing north-westerlies that at 10 or 20 knots can make the return trip something to think about. Nothing of that sort this afternoon, just the prospect of a pleasant tailwind going home, easing me along. The sky clear. Air cool in the hot sun. Smell of sun-hot skin.

*   *   *

108

In falling the willow blocked what could have been the mouth of a stream, but off to one side, what I'd missed on previous trips, is a small break in the cattails—and through it I can see water. I gather speed and slip through, my dog ahead of me unsure of what I'm doing shrinks back from the cattails coming at her from both sides of the canoe, and then we're out into open water, another flowing stream, nearly invisible from the Yahara. Barely ten feet across but deeper than the Yahara, faster flowing and colder. Willows and cattails to the sides, blue sky overhead.

It has rained heavily in the last couple of days, and the surface of Token Creek is filled with bits of mud moving downstream. The river here twists in doglegs around which I sweep in my short and maneuverable canoe, keeping to the inside though not so far as to get hung up on the little sandbars that form on the inside of the curves. I cross one such bar, sweeping around into the new stretch of the creek, and upstream I see that a willow has dropped a branch or two onto the water's surface, so that mud and flotsam is piled up against the upstream side. And it's here that my dog and I see something remarkable.

What it looks like is a kind of underwater flower, about ten of them strung out just upstream of the willow branches and pointing downstream—ten or so flowers the bright orange color of daylilies. And there's a sound like very small pebbles dropping into water. As we drift closer, slowing against the current (I am careful not to paddle, not even to move), I see that these flowers are in fact the mouths of carp just breaking the surface then moving underwater to swallow. These delicate orange flowers are the mouths of feeding carp, huge fish the color of murky water visible just beneath the surface. My dog is watching all this too, she too sees the large fish with complacent faces opening their orange mouths to the creek's surface. While the wind blows uncommonly from the cloudless northeast.

My Father Had a Small Lab

My father had a blood factor named after him—at least in Sweden and until they changed the nomenclature, when it became Factor VII. So to the end of his life my father was glad that people didn't get Alexander's Disease but only a Factor VII deficiency. He told me this one afternoon, we were walking through the park. Rob, he said, did I ever tell you the story about the Swedish Academy? But that's a distortion already, he would never have said a thing like that, never have talked about it unless I'd asked him to: Hey, Pop, did you really have a clotting factor named after you? Why isn't it still called Alexander's Factor?

This was a park he walked through on his way to work, along the Muddy River which forms the border between Brookline and Boston. Fenway Park, close by, is named for this same river or anyway the problems it caused—swamps, mosquitoes—for the first white people in the area. A few times my father brought home turtles that he found along the riverbank. I kept the turtles in the backyard, by the compost pile where there was an ample supply of worms.

So in Sweden, for a while, I suppose, doctors would call each other on the phone to discuss problems of Alexander's Factor. Sometimes doctors called my father asking him what to do before the patient bled to death. My father had a small lab in the basement of the hospital, you could look up through the single window to the metal security grate. It was dark in the lab most times when I visited my father at the end of the day. We'd walk home along the river, and he'd keep his eyes "peeled," as he said, for a turtle to replace the one I'd put back into the river, earlier, on my way over to the hospital.

For Years My Father

For years my father practiced the violin: "What d'ya think, Rob, am I wasting my time sawing away on this hunk of wood?" I would lie on the couch listening to him, New York receding behind the glass panes of the living room. My mother of course had to listen to him play more than I, but she too found it a pleasure, not so much from enjoyment of the sound as from what the sound suggested of the pleasure he was having. Often he said that it was his meditation—trying to play in tune, keep the bow balanced and light—and when he died, at home, he had just finished playing Beethoven's Spring Sonata with his brother Josef. My aunt and uncle had come over for dinner, and after dinner my aunt is talking to my mother—who is keeping rather silent, I think—and my father and my uncle are playing. When they finish the last movement of the Spring Sonata my mother asks my father if he doesn't think it's time to stop, and he smiles and says Yes and dies in the chair where he's sitting, violin and bow still in his hands. Later my uncle tells me that while my father plays, "It's as though he's never been sick."

At Night the Street

At night the street spins webs on the shadows of our room. These patterns shimmer for a moment and then like the ripples of a pond are gone. At the other edge of the pond turtles sun themselves on a log and the weeds flutter.

When the toaster opens, the slice of baked bread slides across the wire mesh. A slight movement. And that's my feeling too, in the moment when the turtles open their eyes, just before they, as paranoid as the next guy, slip into the water.

Worms are pink in puddles along the sidewalk. From across the street there's an earth-and-leaf smell a lot like the park after rain. And while turtles sink to the bottom of the willow pond, ripples disperse on the room's mouth.

Rain

It's raining. Looking out from his second-floor window he can see the roofs of the neighborhood garages, the elms at the other side of his neighbor's yard blowing yellow in the October wind. As if flipping through postcards he can see other rains: the northwoods with their fir and spruce, the smell of the northwoods. . . . And it was raining, yes, it was raining for the sixteenth day out of the last twenty, the clouds still blowing off the gray surface of the lake and the tent getting, as tents quickly do, more and more crowded, sand in the sleeping bags, crud all over everything.

In ten minutes he has to leave for the office, just two blocks away . . . but for now, sipping his fourth cup of coffee of the day, he can sit here thinking about the smoke-filled woods. That summer there'd been a fire in the wildlife refuge and the state was suing the federal government because the fire had spread into the state forest, and every day, unless the wind was blowing off the lake, they could smell the haze. It formed the backdrop on the last little drama of his marriage, he thought to himself. You sure talk a good game, she'd said, one of her last comments before that long silent drive home, the car getting hotter and hotter as they left the northwoods for the wide flat farmlands of the south.

It was raining a moment ago, but now, as if in perfect time for his walk up to the office, it seems to have stopped. Water is dripping off the yellow leaves of the elms and off the birches and spruce of the northwoods. The tent is sagging and there's a smell of smoke in the heavy air. Well I guess I better go make a fire, he says, hunger for a hot meal crawling around in his belly. She is quiet now as if not wanting to make a spuriously nasty comment when there's so much that's substantive that she's only hinted at, though they've been talking all afternoon, rain like distant horses clip-clopping on the tent roof.

As he leaves the house, walking down the creaking bare steps of the front hallway, he realizes it's still drizzling.

*   *   *

They had met when he was still living in the old farmhouse twenty miles outside of town—back, as he used to say later, in the pit of the seventies. It was a cold winter and the wind blew through the thin walls of his northwesterly facing bedroom. He had bought a new carpet and painted the walls a fresh coat of white—and at times it felt like a very cold hotel room that he'd stumbled into in the midst of confusion over whether or not he'd missed the turn in the darkness and was heading off toward Pittsburgh and not, as he'd desired, toward Oil City. He was still teaching school then and she'd drive out in the darkness to be there when he got home. Sometimes they'd drive down to eat at the Penguin, a river cafe with a bar in back that had instead of the usual mirror a panoramic mural of penguins on ice floes sipping margaritas.

By the time they settled into the cold sheets of his bed—her smooth skin warm against his—it would be hours since the sun had set. In some previous ascetic year he had got himself a single bed to sleep in, and all night long they would be forced against the warmth of the other, until it seemed they turned over in unison through the dark country night.

*　　*　　*

It's still raining. From the porch you can look out across the lake at what used to be the Hemingway farm. As a matter of fact Ernest himself delivered groceries, as a kid, to my great-grandfather's family. When he (that is, my great-grandfather) first came up here, and actually for quite a few years after, there weren't any roads around the lake, just a boat from the Foot that, long and mahogany, would bring you around to the silence of the fir and spruce.

There's a road across the lake and at night you can see the headlights from quite a way off, the road dips and rises and the lights fade and reappear. Through darkness the lake laps against the sand. It was an ice-house which my great-grandfather bought and turned into a pine-paneled summer cottage. The trees of course have grown up since then, and the lake is higher than it was—that's a mystery no one's quite figured out. The beach that was more than ten feet wide when people used to wear long bathing suits is now no more than two or three.

And it's still raining. It's rained since we got here, tired of the

114

wet tent, driving through the night and arguing. The one time we stopped was crossing Mackinac Bridge, looking out through the lights and the cables to the broad expanse of darkness. Now we sit on the porch and it rains, rain drips from the pines that my great-grandfather planted and from all the other trees that he didn't. My great-grandfather was born in a small town outside of Cracow and came to Pennsylvania when he was sixteen. Forty years later he bought himself a summer cottage in northern Michigan, and now we sit here, arguing, and it's raining out on my great-grandfather's lake, which, like the clouds, is gray as a trout's belly.

*   *   *

In this dream I'm on a train, it's during the fifties and I'm with some sort of summer camp. The windows are dirty but through them I can see miles and miles of forest. It's only northern Minnesota but to me it may as well be Siberia. The counselors have it in for me, I'm sure, I've heard them at night cracking anti-Semitic jokes.

It's important to get back somewhere but I know that's not where we're headed. That's where she comes into it. Suddenly I'm all the way at the end of the train, in the caboose, only it isn't a caboose it's my old bedroom at the farm and she's in my arms. She's the one in my class I've had fantasies about taking to the two-dollar movie at the Oriental Theatre. In my dream it's as though I'm seventeen again and in love for the first time. She's everything I've ever wished for and besides, it's clear, she loves me too and her hands are all over me. Meanwhile I'm aware how important it is to get the caboose onto the siding and I'm trying to explain this to her but all I can think about is how sweet her hands are and then

The train has stopped and we're all out in the appalling silence of the northwoods. They've told us to set the tents up and that's exactly what everyone is doing but not me. I'm looking around at the gloominess of the rainy day, the brooding trees all around, wondering what happened to her. I'm trying to find her, among all the tents, before I wake up, I know she's around here somewhere. . . .

*   *   *

He would remember it as an autumn of rain. All fall he looked out at the roofs of the East Side and chewed his pencil, before, as he said, really getting down to work. On the shelves of his office the stacks of papers multiplied and the rings his coffee cup made on his desktop were the only sign that every day, raining or not, he would walk the two blocks to work. The air conditioner blew in his face as he sat at his desk. Cold air in the middle of November: it puzzled everyone on his floor of the building.

On the occasional sunny day he would watch the white clouds as they scooted above the roofs and the bare trees, the pale blue sky behind them a sure sign of the colder weather to come. In the middle of all the fir and spruce he had finally let his marriage go, watched it trailing out over the lake like the faint smoke-like trace of geese flying southward. At the first sign of yellow leaves she had left for California, had in fact already written him about her new friend who taught massage at Esalen. She was happy to be far from the "deep freeze of the Midwest," though in northern California, she wrote, the winter rains had already set in.

Ralph Finds a New Park

It's autumn now, it's getting cold. Ralph takes his one-speed bicycle with knobby balloon tires out for a ride this afternoon, his dog runs along beside him. Ralph rides on the dirt trail across the empty field between Milwaukee Street and the railroad tracks—across the grass still green now beneath the wispy October sky. Ralph thinks he'll follow Starkweather Creek, see where it goes before it flows under the tracks and by Olbrich Gardens out to the blue shine of Lake Monona.

Down at the end of Ivy Street Ralph and his dog find a park he's never seen before. The leaves along the edge of the park are green and gold in the October sun. Ralph's dog goes running out across the park as though chasing a deer or a well-thrown frisbee.

And what Ralph's never realized: he sees Starkweather Creek has two branches which flow together here at O.B. Sherry Park. The willow just at the junction of the two streams droops low over the water. Yellow leaves drift slowly on the water's surface. Ralph looks up the curving west branch, trees on both sides touch each other over the middle of the creek. It's like being in the woods, Ralph thinks—and perhaps the deer would be drinking just upstream from him, looking back at him, curious, this October afternoon.

Corn

Just down the street—it's a white house that needs painting. When I walked by this morning on the way to work I saw the corn growing in her backyard. That's when I knew for sure. She came by the other day riding her bike, swooping over to my side of the street and "Hi" as she went by, I thought at first she was talking to my neighbor who was in his yard but "Who's that?" he asked me. "She was smiling at you," he said.

Corn in the backyard. That would be enough for most guys, I suppose I'd be over there knocking on the door, "Hey, I really like your corn, you know I used to live in the country and it's great to see that special sheen on the leaves here in town. I like your smile too." That's how it could be: craning my neck to see into her backyard.

Supermarkets

Supermarkets. I like the long clean aisles of supermarkets: Safeway, Eagle, Sentry—their names likes gods of nutrition. I like the anonymity of supermarkets: I'd drive miles to get to a supermarket where I could be sure of not being recognized. Just last week, as a matter of fact, I saw the ex-wife of a friend who lives in a house where my own ex-wife used to live. We found ourselves at the same time by the frozen food, wisps of fog from the freezer spilling over into the aisle. While she was taking her cans of orange juice I examined the contents list on a bag of Japanese vegetables. And then, not quite brushing her arm, I reached past her and took a can of another, slightly cheaper brand.

Vacation

You go away for a short vacation back East, where the trees are big and the air this time of year has a delicate edge of selenium from the computer companies out along Route 128. It seems to you everyone is coming a little unstuck. You notice new buildings going up fifty or so miles from the center of Boston, squat concrete structures backed into hillsides. All of them face away from the city.

Your return flight is canceled in New York and you are given a ticket back in someone else's name. At the last minute they try to stop him from going on the plane after you "I'm sorry, sir, but you can't go on that plane," you hear behind you—"you see, you've already boarded, and we can't allow your ticket to be used twice."

Stranger still, when you get home. Someone else is living in your apartment; or rather someone else is living where your apartment would be if the building was where you left it just a couple of weeks ago. But there's another building at your address which clearly, what with all the detail around the eaves, is at least a hundred years old. And it isn't what it once was, it hasn't been painted for years. . . .

Fortunately they still recognize you at the bank—but everyone calls you Colonel and people you've never seen before seem to know who you are. "Good show there Colonel," you hear one woman say to you, "I knew you had it in you." When you telephone, none of your friends are in, or their lines have been disconnected. Wandering around in confusion you pass the Army Intelligence laboratory, and as you reach for the doorknob you are quite sure that you've come to the right place.

Garage

It's hard to tell, the picture's all scrunchy and smudged, but it seems like the dictionary defines my garage roof as a "hip" roof—that is, one where the slant changes, like a barn—so I suppose you could say that my garage, sitting back on the southwest corner of my lot, looks like a small barn with even smaller maples growing up all around it (no buds yet, though I've been looking), a lilac, and a couple of hydrangeas or snowball bushes we called them as kids.

Last week I went out there to close the southernmost of the two large doors, which, though its hinges are gone, was flapping in a high wind that brought a blizzard to most of the midwest but fortunately no snow here. You'd best close that door before it gets ripped completely off those hinges, I heard a voice say. Behind the lawnmower disabled now by winter a pallet I'd left for some reason had fallen and was covered with straw. What's straw doing in the middle of the city? This is my story, kid. You think it's easy wintering here with a bit of straw and a pallet separating me from the concrete slab, a roof and some drafty walls. . . .

Right away I knew I'd made a mistake. What's an old man doing in my garage anyway? It would be easy to say it was just the door flapping in the wind, call it a winter breeze. Fortunately the neighborhood was empty. That's right, no one around, that's exactly how it was.

Snow at Ten O'Clock

Leaving the house to walk the dog, I hear what sounds like kids arguing up the block. It's about three and that's when kids walk home from Thoreau and St. Barnard's Schools, still bundled up for winter. It's cloudy—a low ceiling, perhaps a couple of hundred feet; it's drizzling, drops blowing in the northwest wind. . . . Seems like soon it'll rain harder.

But no, it's not kids—low overhead, my god, it's geese!—an irregular V-formation, seems like right over the blue spruce, the geese squawking, arguing back and forth, complaining to each other. I think: geese, it's spring—though the lakes are still frozen. My dog and I walk down along the tracks, and I realize that these geese, they're flying south. . . . What?—southeast, to be precise. This morning I heard on the news: a storm moving in from the northwest. Rain here, north of here snow. Minneapolis, I heard, already has five inches of snow.

I imagine the geese, leaving Illinois early this morning (fog and pale cornstubble in a muddy field), running into snow and a thirty-knot wind coming at them, as the aviators say, at ten o'clock. No wonder they're complaining. It's beginning to rain harder, my dog and I walk back along the tracks. The geese must have turned right around, now they're flying with the wind, flying low, looking for a place to spend the night. I think of the map: perhaps they're heading off toward the marsh at Lake Kegonsa (a straight shot southeast), where white snow and brown cattails surround the open water of Williams Creek.

from *Five Forks:*
Waterloo of the Confederacy

Calhoun's Monument

We go to Charleston for our honeymoon, that city of old brick and ethereal black ironwork—and more beautiful women than I've ever seen in one place before. If Richmond was the Capital of the Confederacy, Charleston was its Heart. Calhoun the Nullifier . . . and a long line of fire-eaters later, Edmund Ruffin lit off the first cannon before the Federal resupply ships could reach the beleaguered garrison at Fort Sumter. (Four years later, just days after Lee's surrender at Appomattox, Edmund Ruffin shot himself—becoming, like Abe Lincoln and so many others, one more casualty of the war.)

Late Sunday morning I drive out to see Fort Moultrie—past azalea and wisteria in bloom, past Krispy Kreme, America's Favorite Doughnuts—where one soft April morning like this in the last century, thousands of shots were fired "to reduce" Fort Sumter, as they used to say in those days. It's a slightly rainy day and I look over the parapet toward Fort Sumter, a low-lying man-made island in the middle of the channel. At dawn, with rose-gold light gracing the clouds and the sand, peace and quiet erupted into hell . . . that would last four interminable years.

It's vacation, so I've lost track of the date, but in fact this rainy Sunday is the anniversary of the opening bombardment, and there's an encampment of Confederate re-enactors set up beside the Fort. I have a brief but vivid fantasy of white men and Asians sitting around a similar scene, years hence, hooches and concertina wire, reenacting the war in Vietnam. On this drizzling morning the re-enactors are sitting around straw-covered dirt, underneath the kitchen tarp, talking low and slow—much as they probably would have done a lot of rainy time during the war: ". . . and not a dang thing anyone can do about it anyhow" drifts by me in a Southern cadence that I find soporific—while the mourning doves' lament breaks the hot stillness of the day. It seems like a long drive back to Charleston and the high-ceilinged antebellum room with full-length windows—shutters closed, already in April, against the heat of the day—and a floor of wide pine planks worn smooth by centuries of bare feet.

Later that afternoon, after the rain has stopped and the sun has come out, we go to see Calhoun's grave, down by the marketplace. But it's Sunday and the cemetery is chained and locked, so all we can do is look through the gate at the large tombstone with CALHOUN written on it, obscured by a huge magnolia and an equally huge live oak bending low over the grave.

We drive to the Calhoun monument near the center of town: there are decaying buildings and, close by, the College of Charleston with its well-scrubbed white kids. Calhoun on his tall pillar, one arm akimbo, looks out over the roofs of lower Charleston toward Battery Park and the Bay. In Marion Park—worn grass and dirt—people down on their luck sit on the benches beneath Calhoun. Across the street the Knights of Columbus and the Soft Rock Cafe. On the pedestal below Calhoun's pillar is written:

TRUTH JUSTICE
and the
CONSTITUTION

I've been reading Whitman's *Specimen Days*, and all day long his sentences have been going through my head:

> I have seen Calhoun's monument. . . . It is the desolated,
> ruin'd south; nearly the whole generation of young men
> between seventeen and thirty destroy'd or maim'd; all
> the old families used up—the rich impoverish'd, the
> plantations cover'd with weeds . . . all that is Calhoun's
> real monument.

At an antiques store downtown we find an antebellum print of Calhoun, a silhouette of the man looking out over a palmettoed landscape from a window with venetian blinds, at the height of his power and prestige, the peak of his self-confidence or arrogance (it depended no doubt on your point of view). I tell the aging couple who own the store—they live in the small apartment upstairs, they inform us, third generation in the antique trade—that it captures the essence of the man. "A few years back they used to talk about pulling him down off his monument and putting up Martin Luther King there," the woman says. "Would've been another War."

*   *   *

The next day at breakfast, we read in the morning paper how a homeowner shot and killed a man running away from an attempted break-in. Elsewhere, this might be considered murder. But the County Sheriff is quoted as saying, "I don't anticipate the Sheriff's Department will make charges." On the back page where the rest of the story is buried, I read that the man killed was black, the shooter white. A City Councilman says, "It's open season on black men."

Postscript

Ralph & the Rabbit

Late may—it's been a cold spring, and the lilacs up and down the block are still in bloom. When Ralph leaves his house to walk the dog, he smells the scent of lilacs along his driveway—stopping to hold one close to his nose, he is ten years old again, in the backyard of his home in Brookline, Mass., dusk falling and his mother on the porch calling him indoors.

Ralph arrives in the park at the end of his street, releases his dog from the leash and she waits expectantly for him to throw a stick. (Soon, he knows, the honey locusts across the street will all bloom at once and the park will be filled with their almost-cloying sweetness—but not quite yet.) Through the trees he can see a small slice of the lake—the wind has died and the waves that have roiled all day are now calm, an hour before sunset. Ralph feels a sudden urge to go canoeing, as he was unable to that morning with the northwest wind breezing up before dawn. There is still, barely, time enough before dark—though his dog is disappointed when, unaccountably, he re-fastens her leash before even once throwing her a stick. He urges her home, not wanting to be out on the water after the sun sets.

*   *   *

As Ralph approaches the limestone bluff in his canoe, the sun is beginning to redden in the northwest sky, still a few degrees above the horizon, casting a yellow light across the lichen-covered stone and the nearly full-leafed trees atop the bluff. The oak leaves are shining with newness and still perfectly-formed like a baby's hand.

At the base of the cliff, the water over many years has hollowed out tiny caves within the rock, and in one of these—a foot across, a foot deep, and half that in height—a movement catches his eye. At first he thinks it's a female mallard, brown feathers against the stone, but there's a flash of white and the motion is too frantic for a duck. As Ralph looks closer he sees a baby rabbit, half submerged in the small waves lapping at the stone. The poor creature is shivering, huddled up against the rock, as the water, after a cold early spring, is not yet forty-five degrees.

In his mind he can see it happen: the rabbit slipping off the top of the bluff, thirty feet up (perhaps chased by a dog) and falling into the water, then swimming toward shore and finding, in the cliff face, a small opening just barely above the waterline. The cliff stretches for many yards each way, and there would have been no place for the bunny to climb ashore. Once there, the rabbit was trapped—crouched on the bottom ledge of the opening, still half under water. It must have happened within the last half hour (while his dog was waiting for him to throw a stick), since the bunnies come out at dusk, and he doesn't think the animal could survive even an hour in the cold water. He's afraid the rabbit will soon succumb to exposure and drown.

"Hang on, bunny," Ralph says aloud. "Help is on the way." He maneuvers the canoe up against the rock wall, though with the undercut at the base of the cliff he's still a couple of feet out from the mouth of the small cave. (Oh shit, he thinks, I'm going to fall in trying to rescue this bunny—and he remembers the story he read years ago in the newspaper about the guy who went fishing with his dog one late fall day, and when the sheriff found the boat it was drifting with a wet dog alone inside. After a searcher found the body along the shore, the coroner surmised that the dog had fallen into the frigid water and the guy had gone in to save it and had a heart attack.) Ralph's canoe is scraping against the limestone and he can see the bunny crouched and shivering at the back of the tiny cave, waves washing across the lower half of his body.

*   *   *

Holding onto the rock with one hand, Ralph slowly shoves the paddle into the little cave, trying to slip it beneath the rabbit. He expects the bunny to shy away, but the creature, perhaps because he's so cold, actually seems to understand what Ralph is trying to do and appears to be trying to hold onto the paddle. But when Ralph starts to pull the paddle back, the bunny (so cold perhaps he can't hold onto the slippery surface of the wood) slips off and starts to sink. Ralph can see small bubbles rising from the nose of the bunny as he slips underwater.

So now Ralph is sure he's going to have to go overboard—but with one last try he pushes the end of the paddle down into the water and tries to get it under the poor drowning bunny. Amazingly, this seems to work. Ralph pulls the paddle back toward himself, and with one hand he manages to grab the bunny. Thankfully the canoe stays upright through this process, since Ralph is crouching down to lower his center of gravity—and in one motion he lifts the rabbit into the boat. The animal is tiny in Ralph's hand, a small thing of fur and bones, shivering and wet.

Ralph puts the paddle down and with his free hand takes from his small backpack of emergency gear the fleece sweatshirt he carries along just in case he capsizes and needs a warm layer of clothing—and he swaddles the bunny with it. The animal doesn't squirm and kick but allows Ralph to wrap it up, placing the bunny so that it faces toward him, and the rabbit is watching him with his large brown eyes. Ralph turns the canoe and starts for home, all the while saying, "You're safe now, Mr. Bunny—such a brave bunny you are, you're going to be all right." (Out of the corner of his eye Ralph sees a boat a short way off with two fishermen, and he figures they must think he's nuts, talking to himself, as they can't see the little head of the rabbit poking through the wrapped-up sweatshirt.)

By the time Ralph gets back to his dock the sun has slipped below the low hills across the lake and the sky is a deep shade of red. Now Ralph has to figure out what to do with the bunny while he takes the boat out of the water and puts it away for the night. He puts the bunny, still wrapped in the fleece sweatshirt, feet first into the backpack, so that only his ears and nose remain visible—and the bunny, still shivering, doesn't resist at all. Perhaps he's still too cold to care, and he stays there watching Ralph take the canoe up along the shore. This done, Ralph picks up the backpack and, cradling it in his arms, walks up the steps toward his house.

*   *   *

Once indoors, the bunny stays in the backpack while Ralph sets up the cage he bought when he first brought his puppy home, a year ago, but has never used. He places the cage in a corner of the living room, puts in a couple of thick folded towels, along with a small bowl of warm milk and a few lettuce leaves. He puts the bunny, still swaddled in fleece

133

and shivering, on the folded towels (and for a moment strokes the bunny's soft ears and murmurs, "You're safe now, little one, safe and warm"), places a blanket over the cage, leaving the front uncovered so the creature can still see out, and goes upstairs to check on the dog and cat.

The cat, a fifteen-year-old tabby, is still sleeping on the bed in the upstairs bedroom, and the dog is hiding under the bed, perhaps afraid of being put in the cage herself. Mission accomplished, Ralph thinks, and lies down to read the book he'd set aside, it seems hours ago, to take his dog for her evening walk. Before long, the book is lying open on Ralph's stomach and he's drifted off to sleep with visions of cold water lapping against limestone and a poor wet creature huddling against the rock.

When Ralph awakens, dusk has turned to night—he can see the lights flickering on the far shore of the lake and there is a small breeze rustling through the oak leaves outside the bedroom window. He goes downstairs to check on the bunny. Carefully he opens the door of the cage. The lettuce leaves appear untouched and the bowl of milk is still full. But right there in the middle of the cage is the rabbit, no longer covered by fleece, but now dry and fluffed up and looking twice the size as before.

Ralph reaches into the cage to stroke the bunny, but the animal, now fully alert and probably terrified, pulls away from his hand and kicks and tries to jump through the cage, actually wedging his head through the small opening between two wire rods. So Ralph quickly closes the door and goes around to the back of the cage to coax and push the bunny back inside, afraid that he might injure himself. This won't do at all, he thinks, He drags the cage over to the front door (carefully, so as not to further alarm the bunny), opens the door and lifts the cage out onto the porch. He then opens the door of the cage to the soft night air. "Good luck, Mr. Bunny," he says, and goes back indoors.

A couple of hours later, taking the dog for her bedtime walk, Ralph sees the lettuce leaves still there in the cage, the milk in the bowl, but the rabbit is gone.

*   *   *

The next evening, as Ralph and his dog return to the house from their evening walk (this time he has spent a good deal of time throwing her a stick in the little park down the street), she starts to pull on the leash, and as Ralph turns he sees a small rabbit on the lawn of the house next door. For a moment or two, before hopping off into the trees, the bunny seems to be looking directly at him.

About the Author

Robert Alexander grew up in Massachusetts. He attended the University of Wisconsin–Madison and for several years taught in the Madison Public Schools. After receiving his Ph.D. from the University of Wisconsin–Milwaukee, he worked for many years as a freelance editor. From 1993 to 2001, he was a contributing editor at New Rivers Press, serving the final two years as New Rivers' creative director. Alexander is the founding editor of the Marie Alexander Poetry Series at White Pine Press. He divides his time between southern Wisconsin and the Upper Peninsula of Michigan.